FIVE WAYS TO BETTER DAYS

A Compendium of Writing and Other Wellness Practices

Patricia McAdoo

ORPEN PRESS

Published by
Orpen Press
Upper Floor, Unit K9
Greenogue Business Park
Rathcoole
Co. Dublin
Ireland

email: info@orpenpress.com
www.orpenpress.com

Paperback ISBN 978-1-78605-073-1
ePub ISBN 978-1-78605-074-8

Printed in Dublin by SPRINTprint Ltd

Five Ways to Better Days

Patricia McAdoo

ABOUT THE AUTHOR

Patricia McAdoo is a psychologist and writer. As a clinical psychologist working in the HSE and NHS for fifteen years, she specialised in the field of primary care and mental health promotion.

She is the author of *Writing for Wellbeing* (Currach Press, 2013) and has facilitated Writing for Wellbeing groups in cancer support centres and for the general public.

She worked as an organisational psychologist, trainer and coach with the Performance Partnership for ten years. Currently she provides mental health awareness and wellbeing training in the corporate sector and is passionate about developing everyday practices to foster wellbeing.

To Dermot, Dominic, Leo and Sam

ACKNOWLEDGEMENTS

I owe a huge debt of gratitude to Marie Murray for her unflagging energy in finding a home for this book and for her endless joy and enthusiasm in steering the ship to safe harbour! And to Orpen Press for being that harbour and especially to Eileen O'Brien for all of her advice and suggestions during the editing of this book. Finally, very special thanks to Dermot Rush and Dominic Rush for taking the time to read the book and for their very helpful feedback.

CONTENTS

Foreword

It is always a privilege to write the foreword to a colleague's book. To do so for this beautiful work, *Five Ways to Better Days*, is a particular delight because of the subject matter of the book and the exceptionally creative, collaborative, user-friendly way in which it is written.

In *Five Ways to Better Days* clinical psychologist, creative writer and author Patricia McAdoo invites readers to live each day in an appreciative way and provides a detailed guide on how to do so. Conjoining positive psychology and creative writing with an amazing array of other beneficial practical interventions, readers are given positive psychology tips, psychotherapy exercises, and creative writing and non-writing ideas and activities designed to deeper their sense of wellbeing and happiness.

Using Patricia's approach, ordinary, everyday beneficial moments are noticed and appreciated. No delight is ignored, no joy unattended, no happiness disregarded and no emotion neglected. In this way, Patricia sets out to ensure that the days that make up our lives are not squandered but are harnessed in the service of health, happiness, mental health and wellbeing, and the development of personal capacity to cope. On the basis that regardless of what happens to us we can retain control over how we respond to life events, this book essentially provides a plan on how to maximise happiness and promote resilience so that our days are better days than they might otherwise be. Every day that is wasted is a day that is lost. *Five Ways to Better Days* reminds us of how precious each day is.

The wealth of ideas, approaches, perspectives and innovations in this book make riveting reading. It is not a book to read in one sitting. It is a book that readers can dip into to find something inspirational to engage or encourage them when they need support. It is also a lifestyle and life-changing workbook: a programme that can be undertaken slowly, gently, persistently and incrementally. It contains an overwhelmingly rich variety of tasks to try, thoughts to think about, routines to consider, questions to answer, dreams to embrace, memories to excavate and emotions to explore. It is philosophy, psychology and practical handbook all rolled into one simple guide to living graciously and coping resiliently with adversity. Not only does Patricia impart the benefit of decades of her own clinical and creative therapy practices, but she generously points readers towards other thinkers and writers in literature, the arts, philosophy, sociology, meditation and mindfulness, narrative psychology, multimodal therapies and the business world. Patricia refers to their research, their writing, their websites and their podcasts and provides readers with these additional resources to increase information, understanding and deep appreciation of life.

In the tradition of positive psychology – with its focus on surplus rather than deficit, positivity rather than pessimism, and building resilience to challenge feelings of defeat – the reader is advised not to ruminate about yesterday nor fear tomorrow but to embrace each day for what it is and savour every second in it. This may sound unrealistically optimistic but from page one this book brings the reader through a respectful process of self-discovery using two key strategies: *anchoring practices* or routines which ground, stabilise and emotionally regulate, and *writing exercises* through which life experiences are articulated. These strategies and others are explored and explained throughout the book. Patricia knows how to help people to harness the therapeutic power of the written word and to recognise their own individual worth, talent and capacity to do so.

From the perspective of narrative therapy our lives are shaped by the stories that are told about us and also those that we tell about ourselves. Add to these the dominant societal discourses that describe people or groups either negatively or positively and we can see how the influence of stories begins in childhood to shape a person's identity or sense of self. Negative narratives weave their way into the heart of a child so that 'problem-saturated' stories can dominate thinking and overshadow the many talents and gifts a person has. This can be reversed. We are hard-wired to tell stories and the neuropsychological benefits of narrating our lives positively rather than negatively are well researched. From the vast literature on narrative psychology there is one simple message – uncover, examine and challenge hostile or dismissive stories and try to find, remember, imagine, create and construct new positive narratives that reflect your giftedness. We can 're-story' our lives. This book helps readers to do that.

So who is this book for? The list is long. It is for anyone who wants to change their life or their view of life in a simple, creative and inexpensive way. It is a book to ignite imagination and uncover personal creativity. It is a resource for therapists and teachers, for psychologists and counsellors, for psychotherapists and practitioners, and for those who wish to integrate writing therapy with positive psychology. It would be beneficial for students on health and social care courses. It is ideal for writing facilitators and creative writing teachers who might like to use the ideas in their work. It is filled with activities that parents might adapt for younger children and it is the ideal book for older children and young adults to try out for themselves. This is a book for those who finally have time to focus on themselves and who want to write about their lives and explore new ways of living. It is a book for those who have no time at all, to remind them to at least catch some moments for self-care. Patricia's book is there to encourage anyone who is anxious or ill because of the psychological benefits that reading such a book and working on the exercises may bring. It is a book for times of sadness and for times of joy, and nobody need ever feel alone or without things to do when this book is beside them.

There is something for everyone in *Five Ways to Better Days*. Whether it is using imagination, reading poetry, writing haiku, becoming absorbed in nature, decluttering physical and mental space, practicing gratitude and kindness, or memoir writing, journaling or autobiographical exercises in which new life narratives are constructed, there is so much in this book. So why not dive into this richness now?

Dr Marie Murray,
Clinical Psychologist, Systemic Psychotherapist and Author
Health Publications and Commissioning Editor, Orpen Press

1

INTRODUCTION

This is a book about days. Specifically, it's about how to have good days by building a set of routines that help to keep you balanced each day no matter what life throws at you. When we wake in the morning, none of us has any real idea of what might happen on any given day, good or bad. We probably have a plan, a rough sketch of how we see things going, but there are no guarantees. The events that happen are not within our control but what we can do is build powerful routines which ground us, make us strong, and foster a sense of wellbeing and happiness.

'How we spend our days is, of course, how we spend our lives.' This quote from the American writer Annie Dillard underlines that what we do on a day-to-day basis defines who we are. And what you do every day matters hugely to how happy you feel; not what you talk about doing some day but right here and now on this day, which is the only guaranteed day you've got. At least 40 per cent of our happiness seems to stem from our own intentional activity rather than genetics or circumstances. In other words, what we choose to do has a significant impact on how we feel. If you feel worn down by a sense of loss or blame or failure, changing your day-to-day routines in a positive direction is a chance to set a new course for yourself.

In his short poem 'Days', Philip Larkin managed to nail all our yearnings for a good life to a simple philosophy of taking each day and making it a happy one. Days are to be happy in, Larkin writes. There is, after all, nothing that we have except this day right here in front of us. No guarantees on tomorrow and all our yesterdays are gone. In his poem Larkin asks where can we live but days? I love the truth of the question. If I had to summarise all of what I have learned as a psychologist, and in my own life, in one sentence it would be this: that day-to-day routines are crucial to happiness, joy, love, accomplishment. It's the stuff of our lives: the regular steady ways in which we commit our time every day, whether that is writing, meditating, exercising, being still, or being with others. What we focus on routinely is what helps bring us a sense of definition: this is who I am, this is what I do. Routine practices help define who we are and who we may become, and the calm steady routines of our day-to-day life help us cope during difficult times.

And yet we often use up our days, perhaps looking backwards, consumed with regret, or fuming in anger and resentment against a grumpy partner who won't cooperate and do what we want. Or we become future-focused, wondering what sort of reaction our selfies will get when we post them or we spend the week just waiting for the weekend. Either way, we throw the day away so lightly. How many times do we wish the day would end? 'I can't wait for this day to be over' we say, or 'this has got to be the very worst day of my life!'

There's a line towards the end of Elizabeth Strout's book *Olive Kitteridge*, when Olive, now a widow in her seventies and living alone, comes to realise something important about her own life: 'it was because she had not known what one should know: that day after day was unconsciously squandered.'

Why then do we throw away our days? Why do we squander our chance to have a really good day? One reason might be that, as research seems to show, we all too easily sail through the day, only half-present, in a sort of trance-like state, lost in our own little world. In an elegant experiment using a smartphone app in 2010, psychologists Matthew Killingsworth and Daniel Gilbert found a clear link between mind wandering (thinking about the past or future) and our experience of happiness. In a time-sampling technique, 2,250 adults were asked two questions at various times during their day: How are you feeling right now? And what are you doing right now? The study found that 46.9 per cent of the time people reported that their minds were wandering, not engaged with what they were doing. And what's really interesting is they rated themselves as less happy when their minds wandered. While mind wandering is something we all do anyway, the clear message from this study is that during the times when we are fully engaged with life we feel happier and that being on automatic pilot, cruising through life in a semi-daze, does not make us happy. We finally arrive exhausted at the end of the day and ask ourselves 'Wow! Where did the day go?' Where indeed?

Positive psychology is a field of research focused on developing actions and routines to see us through tough times and help us foster a sense of optimism and resilience. Having positive emotions broadens our view, helps us see the bigger picture and also encourages us to be more creative. A game-changing moment in psychology happened when Martin Seligman, a highly influential thought leader within the field of psychology, in an address to a major conference of psychologists in 1998, pointed out that psychology urgently needed to focus attention on happiness, wellbeing and resilience as fields of research. In doing so, he and another thought leader, Mihaly Csikszentmihalyi, encouraged researchers to ask a new question: what are all the people who are coping well *doing* to foster their own resilience?

Instead of letting our days slip through our fingers, we can make them days to be happy in, days which we spend well, not squandered but truly lived well. And that is what this book is about: how to have good days through anchoring practices and writing exercises in each of five areas of personal strength, which encourage you to practice being more grateful, more tolerant, fully engaged and focused in flow activities, clear on what values are important to you, and connected to other people. These five key themes have been found to be core to happiness in the research emanating from the field of positive psychology.

Anchoring Practices

Anchoring practices are practices which help us to hold tight during times of trial and calm us when times are tough. They may help you to change the direction of your own story, to enhance your sense of wellbeing, and to broaden and build your sense of yourself as a strong, resilient person who can weather the tough times when they come. These anchoring practices can be ways to ground yourself no matter what else is going on in your life, a set of routines or practices which will steady the ship during stormy times. Not every day is going to be a good one. Tragedies happen. People get ill, break up, lose their jobs. The importance of our positive routines cannot be overestimated in getting us through a rocky patch. When you feel tossed on a stormy sea, knowing that every day you will walk in nature can be the thing that buoys you up.

We can't do much about the events that shape our lives, but we can determine our own response to what happens to us and our responses can re-shape even negative events in unexpected, interesting and therapeutic ways. The writer Marian Keyes wrote a book of baking recipes because she had found that baking complicated new cakes helped to get her through a time of severe depression. What may have been so powerful about baking for her was what many people who love baking or following new recipes describe: they forget everything else as they become wholly absorbed in following a new and complicated recipe. That is the experience of flow, a key aspect of positive psychology which we will look at in Chapter 4. Anchoring practices – developing positive routines – are the first key way to change your own story day by day in a more positive direction.

Expressive Writing

The second key way to redefine your own story is to write about it and use this as a way of reflecting on where you have come from, where you are now and then looking at all the future possibilities ahead. Negative stories are not irreversible. Standing back and reflecting on our stories can help set us free.

In 2003 David Isay founded StoryCorps when he placed a story booth in Grand Central Station, New York to allow people the opportunity to record their story. The focus of StoryCorps is an interview which records a conversation. Five books later, and with many more story booths and a dedicated app, StoryCorps has pretty much proved its point about how much people value the opportunity to tell their story. StoryCorps has also fostered greater understanding and connectedness between people of all sorts of backgrounds and ethnicities.

So, as StoryCorps has shown, we often have a dominant story in our lives. This dominant story may be solution-focused or problem-focused. We may see ourselves as competent and able to deal with what happens to us, or we may see ourselves as unable to cope, fearful of success or anxious in our relationships. For example, how often have you heard a highly successful person mentioning someone in their early life, a parent or teacher, who emphatically believed that they could be anything they wanted to be, that the sky was the limit in terms of possibilities? The story which was absorbed from this encounter was one of personal strength and inner resilience, and this story was then internalised and served them well as a working model of who they were as a person.

In the experiment referred to earlier in this chapter, participants were found to spend almost half their time mind wandering, leading them to feel less happy. What are we actually doing then on automatic pilot? When we disengage from the present moment to go on a mind wander, we weave stories about what happened to us in the past or we fantasise about what might happen in the future. Very often we repeat the same story over and over on a loop. Part of a therapist's job is to excavate the kinds of stories we repeat on a loop, especially the negative ones. In other words, what are the core beliefs we have picked up about ourselves from these stories that we tell ourselves over and over?

Mind wandering can lead us into a vortex of stories that we are not at all conscious of and yet which often make us unhappy, feeling trapped, lost and powerless. What if the stories you grew up with were negative ones? What if you were told 'you'll never make the grade'? That sort of story might just fire you up to prove the person who handed you this version of yourself wrong, but it could easily hem you in, filling you with doubt and a lack of entitlement. This is the power that stories have, and in our day-to-day mind wanderings our lives are told by them.

Imagine you're about to face a big exam and you don't have a good history with exams. Your mind wanders back to scenes in previous exams, your hand shaking so badly you could barely hold the pen, your mind a blur of swimming facts, all jumbled up, your head feeling hot. You see again that look of disappointment on your mother's face the day you told her your results. You imagine the first day of the exam you're now facing into. You probably haven't slept well. You are tired, your brain is fuzzy. None of your favourite poets are on the paper. In fact, you haven't studied any of the ones that have come up. This is a disaster. You leave early. You fail. These mind wanderings, both backwards to the past and forwards to events yet to come, are all telling a story of failure and anxiety, of not being good enough. And it's likely that by the time you actually do face the exam, fired up with these negative stories repeated over and over, your body will flood with anxiety.

Or you have a date, with someone you met the previous weekend. Someone you don't know. Your mind wanders back to a year ago, to the night when your ex-girlfriend broke up with you. It was your first proper relationship. You had always been very shy and found it hard to start conversations with girls. So you were thrilled when at last you met someone. But after a few weeks together with this girl she told you she realised that she had nothing in common with you. She mentioned being bored, wanting more. You replay that scene in your head, then the aftermath of the days that followed the break-up. Now you feel swamped with sadness. Your mind jumps again, this time to your plans for the weekend. You start to imagine the whole thing going really badly wrong. You might run out of things to say. You imagine yourself struggling to find the right words. You get nervous. Maybe you should give it a miss, cancel or just not show up.

Reflecting on how you are portrayed in the stories you tell yourself can reveal a lot about how you see yourself:

- Are you a hero? Someone who 'saved the day'?
- Is there a victim in the story and, if so, are you that person?
- Are you a leader or a follower?
- Who is to blame in the story? Who is the fall guy?
- Do you fail or succeed?
- Are you lost in the story, not knowing what to do?
- Do you feel trapped by your own story?
- Does the central story of your life suggest a promising future cut short or a series of missed opportunities?
- Do you see yourself as someone who is always full of enthusiasm for each new venture but then runs out of steam: someone who tried 'a hundred different things' but never stuck at any one thing?

Through writing it is possible to widen the margins of the story you have about yourself to see the richness there, that somehow you have endured through tough times and you have learned from your difficulties. Expressive writing is a way to write your own story, to understand it in a rich and deeper sense; writing can heal the hurt of past stories and help us escape the tyranny of stories we feel bound by.

In expressive writing people are actively encouraged to break free of stories that are creating problems for them and to widen their perspective to include new and different versions instead. The notion of 'versions' fits very well with contemporary thinking about identity in psychology: that there is not just one self, but many versions of ourselves.

While most researchers in the field of expressive writing come from a psychological perspective, many of the leading practitioners in the field approach the topic from a more literary perspective, as writers and poets. In a way, this is surprising because psychologists tend to develop their practice based on the research available so there is usually a direct and logical relationship between practice and theory. It just so happens that leading practitioners in the field of expressive writing do not in fact come from a psychological background. Therefore, the methods that have evolved over the past thirty years are based on a rich blend of using imagery and metaphor as key bridges to encourage participants to re-imagine their story. And so there is, to some extent, a gap between the psychological theories that demonstrate the efficacy of the approach and the very wide diversity of approaches now used in the field.

In fact, I think this disjointed development has led to a wonderfully rich variety of approaches. This is central to why the techniques are so effective because instead of asking people to write directly about events, the use of imagery and metaphor encourages people to write at a different angle – at a slant – and writing 'slant' helps to fire the imagination. It lets people write about sometimes painful areas of their lives in a positive and transformative way. And writing is not only free, you can do it anytime, anywhere. It's one of those go-to activities that you can just do – no preparation required, no forethought: just you and the empty page.

The Five Ways to Better Days

There are five key methods of resilience development discussed in this book:

- Deeply appreciating
- Flow
- Thinking flexibly
- Values and goals
- Connections

Deeply Appreciating

Robert Emmons, a leading researcher on gratitude, in his book *Thanks*, says, 'If you want to sleep more soundly, count blessings not sheep.' There has been an abundance of studies on the importance of articulating our gratitude for things that have occurred, for people who have been supportive, or for moments or events that have lifted our spirits. Saying thanks, writing down our gratitude, is psychologically significant, and in this chapter we go beyond the normally prescribed process of simply making lists of things for which we are grateful to look at many other ways to express deep appreciation.

Flow

In his book *Flow: The Psychology of Happiness*, the psychologist Mihaly Csikszentmihalyi described a state of 'flow' based on interviews with thousands of people from diverse backgrounds, including ballet dancers, tennis professionals, chess players and surgeons. The flow state happens when we are engaged in an activity in which:

- The activity itself is intrinsically rewarding
- We are clear on what is required
- We are concentrating fully to the extent that we lose awareness of ourselves
- There is no worry about failure
- Time is transformed so we 'lose all sense of time'
- Actions and awareness are merged

In this chapter we look at how to deepen your own experience of flow and how to use free writing as a way to induce a flow state.

Thinking Flexibly

Through changing perspectives we see ourselves and others with more compassion; we are no longer locked into one way of seeing things; we move away from our own egocentric view; we develop flexibility and tolerance; and we widen the lens of our experience. Changing perspective helps us see that we don't have to believe that inner voice that keeps telling us the same story about our life repeatedly, that there are other, more positive, ways of seeing our story. Changing perspective is a cornerstone technique of expressive writing as we explore other aspects of ourselves through guided imagery and meet our inner mentor.

Values and Goals

It can be very helpful to step back now and again and look at the big picture. Where are you going? What are your values? This can certainly help with putting a meaningful structure on our days, which otherwise can feel like they are drifting away and that 'we get nothing done!'

If you write down your goals rather than just think about what it is you want to do you are much more likely to achieve them. This type of writing can sharpen your focus on what really matters to you.

Connections

The value of having close relationships in our lives has been found to be key to personal happiness. This chapter is about figuring out the issues we may have in our close connections with others, including appreciating what we have gained or lost over the course of our life.

***

As you can see, this book is all about practice, about ways of building anchoring routines and using writing techniques which on a day-to-day basis improve your sense of wellbeing. In each of the five chapters a range of anchoring practices and writing exercises are provided. The book provides a roadmap to both anchoring practices and writing exercises with which you can experiment, dipping in and out of them, and see what suits you best. Finally, ideas on resources for each chapter which you may find helpful are provided at the end of the book.

Who Is This Book Aimed At?

This book is for anyone who wants a practical guide to wellbeing using well-researched methods. It is also useful for those who work in the field of personal change:

- Coaches
- Therapists

- Counsellors
- Psychologists
- Mental health professionals

The techniques presented here can and are used in team settings within organisations and in reflective practice for health and social care practitioners.

While the health benefits of expressive writing are well-documented, there are also benefits for writers of fiction and non-fiction, and many writers and creative writing groups use methods like these to give their writing a kick-start. In the resources section at the end of this book several books are mentioned which focus on the benefits of free writing, for example as a good basis for any other type of writing.

Chapter 2 is specifically written to shine a light on the background to expressive writing. But, of course, you can manage all the writing exercises in the book perfectly well without reading it so do skip right on if this doesn't interest you.

I hope that this roadmap helps you on your own unique journey to better days.

2

WHY WRITE?

Many of us carry baggage when it comes to expressing ourselves through the medium of pen and paper. We associate writing with the dreaded school essay or college assignment – in other words with work. In the back of our minds we may see the red slashes of the teacher's comments across our efforts. We may be fearful of failing. But expressive writing is not that kind of writing. It is heart writing and, as a result, the writing is emotionally eloquent. It sings. There is a real sense of truth that shines through with which other people in a writing group easily connect. There may be a nod of recognition or a murmur of approval or laughter at a humorous description. Sometimes there is just sheer awe at the clarity of the writing. And people shine in writing groups as they see that they are in fact not only able to write but that their writing has managed to capture something deep and precious.

How Does Expressive Writing Work?

One of the most prolific researchers in the field of expressive writing, Professor James Pennebaker, describes how writing forces people to stop what they are doing and briefly reflect on their lives. He notes that when people write in a way that helps them to organise their story into a more coherent narrative, they tend to use sentences like: 'I now realise that ...' or 'I understand why ...'. In other words, they have gained some insight into events and made sense of them in a way that perhaps allows them to move on with their lives. Such writing is a way of getting a fresh perspective or take on our life, to see where we are, where we have been and where we may go in the future.

What Does the Research Say about the Benefits of Writing?

In the early 1990s, James Pennebaker began a psychological experiment which both he and many other researchers continue to research in various forms to this day. The experimenters asked people to write for twenty minutes for three or four consecutive days about the worst thing that ever happened to them. Pennebaker found that this simple experiment conclusively led to positive effects on a whole range of health indicators. The studies of Pennebaker over the past thirty years and of other researchers have consistently shown that participants who wrote about traumatic, stressful or emotional events visited their doctor less, had stronger immune systems and suffered from fewer colds and flus. While the writing times were short, participants reported thinking and dreaming about their writing. As Pennebaker pointed out, participants were psychologically in the experiment 24 hours a day for several days. The study concluded that writing about distressing events helped participants make sense of the events and reduce distress.

These writing exercises offered participants an opportunity to stand back from traumatic experiences which they may have previously tried to bury or forget. The exercises asked them to make sense of what had happened. Even more importantly, participants were given an opportunity to reframe these experiences in a different and more positive light by examining 'what I learned from this was ...'.

The people who gained most from the experience were those who could sift through all the jumble of feelings, develop a coherent story and find some meaning in what had happened to them – not always an easy thing to do, and, if events have been deeply traumatic, some people may need counsellor support as they undertake it. Four months after the original experiment, the participants were asked what the experience had meant to them and their responses were overwhelmingly positive. They described how they were finally able to deal with what they had experienced and work through the pain instead of blocking it out, so that the experience could be put to rest and not be painful when they thought about it. Writing about their feelings helped them understand their own reactions and why they had felt that way.

This finding has been replicated across age, gender, culture, social class, and personality type in hundreds of studies over the past four decades. A study in New Zealand in 2017 found that when people wrote about their thoughts and feelings for just twenty minutes three days in a row two weeks before a skin biopsy their wounds healed quicker than those of a control group.

Expressive writing helps to sort out your thoughts and feelings and develop a sense of mental space and order;

to puzzle out what is happening; and to escape the traps and chains of old thoughts and ideas. The point is that you are not just carried along as a passenger in your own story. This is your autobiography that you are living. You get to be the author not of the events that happen to you, perhaps, but of how you react to them, how you make sense of them, how you incorporate these events into your story. Throughout this book you will be invited to excavate and uncover all the creative capacities hidden within you that you may not know you have or that you may have neglected within yourself. Through the magic of writing you will be able to give yourself and your life the expression it deserves.

How to Develop a Writing Practice and What to Expect

There is habitual writing and once-off writing, and both have their benefits. There may be times of great emotional intensity when you write furiously for a few days or hours, and times when you are chugging along with your writing practice in the background of your life. Ongoing writing practices introduce a cadence and rhythm to your life and these positive, predictable milestones become part of the ebb and flow of your life in a good way. Different types of writing may happen at different times of the day, from free-flow limbering-up writing, which some people like to do in the morning, to end-of-day writing, which might involve expressing gratitude and appreciation of the good aspects of that day.

There are both structured and unstructured exercises here. Tight structures give people a chance to express themselves in ways that might surprise. For example, you may be asked to choose the six words of your memoir but which ones to choose? Now that is a challenge! Alpha poems, in which each line begins with a specific letter of the alphabet, seem impossible at the beginning, but people quickly adjust and enjoy the challenge; they relish the rules by which to write. Structure sets you free instead of smothering your creativity.

Metaphor, imagery and perspective are all key tools to unlock your thoughts and feelings. They set us free when we are frozen. They give us permission to fly above the ground and see things anew. Poetry can also be a very big part of expressive writing; poems instantly touch a chord. The essence of an expressive writing exercise should be that it forces you out of your comfort zone but gives you confidence that you can deal with the task and fires you with enthusiasm to relish what is coming next.

Your writing will surprise you. What you do in expressive writing is to dive deep and from the moment of departure the excitement builds. You start at the top of the slippery slope with your nice shiny paper and heaven knows where you will end up. Reading back over what you have written with love and an open heart is very important. And when you read back to yourself you may be amazed by what happens. People in writing groups often look up blinking as if they have been in a dream: 'did that really happen?' You might find yourself laughing out loud at 'things you have come up with'. Over time you will get more familiar with the writing side of yourself or what might be called the 'you' that is doing the writing. This may be a part of yourself you may not have encountered much before.

Expressive writing is fun, and it is interesting because we are endlessly absorbed by the story of our own life. Nobody ever needs to read what you have written, and in the writing groups which I facilitate nobody ever does.

But when people read aloud their own writing and when they see the pleasure that other people get from what they have written, they blossom in terms of confidence.

You don't need to write every day, though you may want to. I think it's important to state that at the outset. This is not one of those books that forces daily practice as the only way to develop your ability to write. It would be a real shame if your writing became another daily chore, something more you must add to the to-do list. If every time you see your notebook you feel an inward groan of guilt that 'you should get back to it', then it's not serving its purpose. Writing should be a safe and enjoyable activity, something to come home to, like a good friend you can rely on to always be there; something to dive into, to get lost in; something just for you.

The purpose of writing is to be something useful, a background presence in your life, to fall into, to fall back on. It's a lovely, precious resource that hopefully you will treasure and one day you'll see that you have filled a whole notebook with your writing.

Start to think about when, where and how you might like to write. Setting your intention to write in this way is an important first step. It can help a lot to have a nice notebook which is just for your writing if you have decided to write longhand, or to set up a special folder if you have decided to use your computer. You might also give some thought to the times and places that are likely to suit you without being too prescriptive about this – just more of a general idea of when it's likely that you can make space in your day for writing and finding a spot where you can write with fewer interruptions.

I would encourage you not to get too hung up on any rules at all about writing or having the perfect conditions for writing. Though there may be a favourite time for you to write or a favourite chair to sit in while you write, the more specific you become about the perfect writing conditions the less enjoyable the entire process is because conditions are rarely as perfect as we would like. Phones ring; people interrupt. The real beauty of expressive writing is it can be done anywhere at all at any old time: middle of the night writing is wonderful if you can't sleep and you want to figure things out or write down all your present worries so you can perhaps go back to sleep, happy that they are all stored on a page beside your bed and not whizzing round your brain anymore.

I've seen people write wonderfully under the most difficult of circumstances. I remember watching in awe someone who was gravely ill coming to a writing group accompanied by nurses and an oxygen tank. She had barely sat down at the table and begun to write when a family member interrupted the session with some request for her. My admiration grew as I watched her quietly and serenely return to the writing task and then go on to produce a stunning piece of writing which drew admiration from everyone else there that day. I wonder if we tend to write our best work in such trying circumstances. Challenges often ignite us. Runners head out into the rain and the wind, such is the draw of the open road. They don't wait for perfectly dry conditions. So too we writers pick up our notebooks, perhaps in a crowded railway station or a prison cell or a hospice, and write. If you want to write, just write. It's that simple.

Getting Support

Writing, above all, should be something you love, an oasis within your day, though, of course, sometimes the writing itself may throw up difficult issues. There is no doubt that expressive writing can evoke painful memories. The evidence from research is that when people do write about painful topics they often feel worse immediately afterwards but then they may begin to feel better in the days and weeks that follow. If you're writing about deeply hidden topics that you haven't explored much before, consider looking for support from a good friend or a counsellor.

In my experience of facilitating many writing groups over the years I have rarely, if at all, come across situations where someone wrote about issues in a way that was too much, too upsetting, too difficult to deal with. In fact, because we are the people doing the writing, we tend to be guided by our own judgement in terms of what we can deal with at any given time. That said, if you find that your writing is leading you into difficult and painful areas of your life and it is all becoming too much then stop. Talk to someone you trust; share what you have written if this feels like the right thing to do for you. Return to the writing itself only when you feel ready. And, as noted already, do consider getting some support in the form of a good friend to talk to or professional help by talking to a therapist. Your writing may prove to be a very useful resource in therapy and many therapists encourage clients to write.

One of the ways to write about difficult issues is through metaphor or by taking someone else's viewpoint. So, for example, painful episodes in childhood can be written from the viewpoint of a faithful childhood companion such as a doll or teddy bear. Writing at an angle, or writing 'slant', about difficult experiences can be useful and there are plenty of such writing exercises later in this book.

Don't Write Yourself into a Vortex

There is a danger with expressive writing that you can end up writing about the same issue day after day and in the same way. Remember that the people in the expressive writing research who were found to get the most benefit were the people who over the course of a few writing episodes found that they gained some insight into their story. It made sense to them and then they were able to move on.

If you find yourself getting stuck in the same writing loop all the time, I would encourage you to try something different, particularly to try writing something shorter and with a tight structure. For example, writing only for a specific period of time or trying something new, something outside your own comfort routine as a writer – like writing a haiku (a Japanese poem of seventeen syllables, in three lines of five, seven, and five). Or you may wish to write a six-word memoir, which condenses and encapsulates powerful moments and emotions in carefully chosen words such as the famous six-word story by writer Ernest Hemingway, which said, simply and poignantly, 'for sale, baby shoes, never worn'. Writing within such a short structure may help to shake up your writing into new and creative styles and help you gain a greater sense of perspective. In so doing, it may help you move on.

And so I hope that you discover through the writing practices a sense of the joy of writing, an insight into your own story and an ability to write your way to become your best self.

3

DEEPLY APPRECIATING:
THE BENEFITS OF GIVING THANKS

'There are thousands of ways to kneel and kiss the ground',
Rumi.

Have you heard about the invisible gorilla? In a clever experiment, psychologists Daniel Simons and Christopher Chabris illustrated that when people are asked to pay attention to one thing (counting ball passes between players in a basketball game) at least half of them did not see a person in a gorilla suit walk slowly across the court between the players. While it may not matter too much whether we see a passing gorilla in a psychology experiment, it matters a great deal to our subjective experience of our life if we constantly fail to pay attention to good things that happen to us.

It's so easy to squander time, not pay attention to what is going on, and not fully appreciate the moments in our lives. We have a strong and ancient negativity bias in our brains dating back to hunter-gatherer days when it served our species well to be highly attuned to the threat of physical danger. So being able to fight other predators or run away quickly was a skill we couldn't afford to be without and our brains became hardwired to notice and respond to negative events more than positive ones because it mattered more that we could make quick and intelligent fight or flight decisions under threat from danger. However, we still have this brain that is hardwired in terms of a negativity bias and therefore we tend to adopt a fight or flight response when faced with what we perceive as threats even though we are not in any physical danger. Our fight or flight response is triggered by all kinds of stressors, like having to make a speech, dealing with heavy traffic, being late or feeling criticised.

At the end of every day are you the sort of person who tosses and turns trying to sleep? Do you find yourself replaying all the things that went wrong, all the things you didn't get around to doing, gnawing your way through a ton of worries? Our natural hunter-gatherer default mode of operating is to be wary and watchful for the things that could potentially go wrong for us. This was all very well when we had to ward off other species but doesn't serve us so well in the environment in which we find ourselves now. Our antennae are finely tuned to pick out the bad things that happen to us but perhaps to overlook the good.

The natural tendency of the brain is to have a kind of low-grade refrigerator hum of anxiety. However, neurons that fire together wire together, meaning that pathways in the brain are formed and reinforced through repetition. So, we can alter the structure of our brain by paying attention to positive experiences. And, in order to overcome this hardwired negativity bias in our brains, we have to actively swerve our brains away from fight or flight mode in the direction of noticing positive experiences.

This chapter is all about reversing that phenomenon of looking at where things go wrong in our lives by developing an active practice of looking for and deeply appreciating the good things that happen to us. In his book *Giving Thanks*, Robert Emmons, a professor of psychology at University of California, and the psychologist who has led research into gratitude since 1998, describes how, together with Michael McCullough, he discovered that there is no 'set point' to happiness and that when people regularly practice gratitude in their lives not only do they experience a much greater and often life-transforming sense of wellbeing and satisfaction, but their partners, family and friends notice that the person is also more pleasant to be around and happier.

Happy people tend to feel an abundance of joy. They feel content and that life has meaning. They have a sense of purpose. Unhappy people tend to have fewer satisfying relationships and feel less grateful in their lives. In terms of character strengths that contribute to wellbeing, gratitude is among the most beneficial.

Being grateful is about appreciating, being thankful and having a sense of wonder about what life can offer. Numerous studies on gratitude indicate that being grateful contributes to life satisfaction, happiness and a sense of wellbeing, and that this gratitude tends to centre on an appreciation of the simpler things in life.

Emmons describes the two aspects to gratitude as being firstly an acknowledgment of the goodness in our life. This acknowledgment can mean we adopt a different perspective. For example, we suddenly see that out of a difficult experience we learned something new or gained a different insight and we are grateful for this. Secondly, we also recognise that at least some of this goodness stems from outside ourselves. Acts of kindness to others also contribute to personal happiness. Repeated acts of kindness over a period of time seem to build up happiness levels in a sustained way. Such a finding suggests that happiness can be boosted through sustained and intentional gratitude-oriented activities. The exercises in this chapter focus on paying attention to the everyday moments of our lives in order to seek out the good aspects of tiny moments throughout our day.

Anchoring Practices

Spend Time in Nature

There is an emerging evidence base for the physiological and psychological benefits of what the Japanese call forest bathing. If you spend a lot of your time sitting in front of a screen and immersed in a relatively noisy environment, then the peace, stillness and silence of a green space like a wood, forest trail or city garden could be just the thing to lower your stress levels and help you to see literally 'the bigger picture'. One of the psychological benefits of green spaces is that they induce in us a sense of awe due to the power and beauty of nature. Forest bathing is often described as an immersive experience, as if the world vanishes as we immerse ourselves wholly in the experience of nature. We are no longer looking 'at' a view but instead we are part of it all, soaking up the experience from the inside out.

Doctor Jane Goodall, who devoted much of her life to studying chimpanzees and who founded the Ngamba Island Chimpanzee Sanctuary, spent a great deal of time among the chimpanzees in the rainforests of Tanzania. She says that for her being in the forest is the most spiritual place on the planet: 'you get a very strong feeling of the interconnectedness of living things. It's really magical for me'.

> Try widening your perspective by immersing yourself in a green environment.

Taking in the Good

Try watching Rick Hanson's short talk 'Taking in the Good' in which he describes a simple practice to savour present moments. He is the author of the *Buddha Brain* blog and his website is full of interesting ideas about staying in the present moment. Like squirrels storing up nuts for winter, we can store up good experiences in our memory to savour during hard or stressful times. We can store up such positive experiences and find our way back to them to enhance our sense of contentment and wellbeing. He shows how we can deepen our experience of positive events by paying attention in a more heightened way.

> Extend the experience of something good by not just jumping onto something else. Notice that the positive experience is soaking into your brain. Take up to fifteen or twenty seconds to do this while relaxing your body and absorbing the positive experience. The 'something good' could be anything from looking at a clear blue sky to the sound of the wind whispering through trees or looking into your baby's eyes.

Mindfulness

As we saw in Chapter 1, researchers found that people spent 47 per cent of their time on automatic pilot, where they drifted away from the present to thinking about the past or the future. They also found that when people reported that they were on automatic pilot they also felt less happy. So, mindfulness matters in terms of our happiness.

Mindfulness is beneficial in the following ways:

- It helps us be more present in our own life in an everyday sort of way so that we tend to drift away less into automatic pilot (that feeling of drifting along and wondering where did the day go).
- It slows us down, reawakens our sense of wonder, makes us more aware.
- It helps us to reconnect with real life moment by moment instead of getting side-tracked with phones and other electronic devices.
- It makes us more deeply appreciative of what we have here and now, today, instead of walking through our life in a shutdown state of mind.
- It sharpens our sense of observation, which every good writer needs.

> You could try meditating as a way of focusing on the now in a very deliberate way. Tara Brach is a clinical psychologist and meditation teacher and she has many different guided meditations on her website *(www.tarabrach.com)* with meditations covering many different themes and of different lengths.

Savour the Moment

In the introduction to his book, *A Monk's Guide to a Clean House and Mind*, Shin Buddhist monk Shoukei Matsumoto points out that we are each composed of the very actions we take in life so acting conscientiously with even the simplest tasks is a habit worth forming. In Japanese

Buddhism cleaning is revered as a way to cultivate the mind: '*Zengosaidan* is a Zen expression that we must put all our efforts into each day so we have no regrets, and that we must not grieve for the past or worry about the future.' In a way, simple cleaning rituals, done with attention, go to the heart of what his book is about: living each day with intention, enjoying it fully and savouring the moments.

Focus your attention each day on one simple activity like washing dishes, brushing your teeth or cooking a meal. Really savour every moment of it as if you were doing it for the first or last time.

Self-Compassion

The ability to be kind to ourselves is important as it helps keep us anchored when we hit a rocky patch, but it is also good for our brains. The results of a study carried out using imaging techniques in 2014 found that people with low self-esteem had reduced grey matter volume in brain regions known to support emotional self-regulation in response to stress.

There are many guided meditations on self-compassion. Tara Brach's website is a good start.

Speaking Kindly about Yourself

If you find that you regularly pepper your conversations with negative expressions about yourself then why not practice doing the opposite?

Try saying something good about yourself, acknowledging what you did well or express satisfaction at a job well done.

Even if you have difficulty saying this out loud, say it quietly to yourself.

Savouring the Days

In the 2013 British film *About Time*, a father and son can travel back in time but the main lesson that the son learns is to try to live each day as if it was the final day of his life.

A good practice to try is not only to write what it is that you're grateful for at the end of each day but also pay that gratitude forward by mindfully waking up to the good experiences as they happen, the small day-to-day encounters with others which you can influence and make even better.

Acknowledgment

Acknowledging the good things that others do is a way of pausing and paying attention, of bowing in the face of such expressions of kindness; and the more we do it, the easier it becomes to do.

Try looking for the kind of opportunities that arise in the day-to-day encounters we have with other people. Look for times to stop and thank someone – for example your friend for buying you a coffee, a shop assistant for offering helpful advice when you're trying to decide on a gift for someone, or a colleague who smiles when you come in to work.

Self-Soothing

One of the most important skills we can learn in life is the ability to self-soothe. This helps us see that we have something to hold onto in times of difficulty as well as things we enjoy on an everyday basis.

What is it about what you enjoy doing, possibly something you do every day or every few days but at least on a regular basis? It might be a daily walk, doing a crossword, going for a swim or reading in bed. Having a heightened awareness of our own ability to self-soothe with regular practices that we enjoy gives us a greater feeling of resilience and competence and a belief that we can weather the storms when they come.

Create a Space that Gives You Joy

A friend of mine has made her front porch a sun-filled oasis of peace and tranquillity. Like with many country houses in Ireland, anyone who calls to see her uses the back door and so she converted the front porch, with its lovely sea view, into a little sanctuary to read in and daydream, and sometimes to entertain visitors in with its comfortable cushioned seating area and rugs for when it's cold.

Create your own space. It's good to know that at any time, especially when you've had a tough day, you can retreat to a little corner of the world, a place to be happy in or calm and content, to curl up in with a cup of tea, a book or a glass of wine. This could be a favourite chair by a window, a sunny space in your home, a room with a lovely view of a tree, or a quiet comfortable corner on winter evenings with a candle, colourful cushions and a favourite rug.

Writing and Gratitude

The aim of expressive writing is to heighten our own awareness, to pay attention to what is going on, and to be more fully present to our life. Writing about being grateful has the following benefits:

- Gratitude is a valuable resource but being silently grateful does not appear to be as useful as expressing this gratitude through writing.
- Gratitude has a significant impact on wellbeing. People who keep a gratitude journal are more optimistic and feel happier. They report fewer physical problems, sleep better at night and wake up feeling more refreshed. They are likely to spend more time exercising. Robert Emmons and Michael McCullough asked people with neuromuscular disorders to make nightly lists of things for which they were grateful. After three weeks, participants reported getting longer, more refreshing sleep.
- Gratitude helps you to notice the good things and helps you see patterns in terms of what aspects of your life keep coming up in the gratitude list: maybe walking the dog or getting to bed early. You begin to pay attention to the things in your life that you consistently value and, even better, you begin to appreciate that the best things in life really are free.
- You notice that there is an ebb and flow to the good and the bad times. Being grateful builds our resilience. By having consciously paid attention to noticing and writing about positive experiences, it is easier to draw on these memories as a buffer in challenging times.
- Grateful people are more likely to seek out help or support when they feel they need it. They are also more likely to adopt a positive approach to solving a difficulty than simply avoiding it.

- You also see that it's the little things, like someone being particularly nice to you, that you notice. After a while, you begin to bring more of that into your life because you appreciate it and you notice it more, so it becomes a self-fulfilling prophecy in a good way. You begin to mirror back to yourself what you're grateful for especially and to understand that it's often the small things people do for you and, even more importantly, you become grateful to yourself for handling things better than you did before.
- You become kinder in your relationships with other people. Researcher Barbara Fredrickson describes the link between gratitude and kindness: 'Gratitude creates the urge to creatively consider new ways to be kind and generous oneself. The durable resources accrued when people act on this urge are new skills for expressing kindness and care to others.'
- Making a short list of things for which you are grateful changes your perspective to one of focusing on the positive aspects of your day and not chewing over the negative aspects. So being grateful builds on what we will cover later in this book: perspective-taking. Practising gratitude is about shifting your perspective in a deliberate way to look for the good things and not the bad things that happen to you. Having a regular and deliberate practice to notice good events changes us in ways that can be sustained throughout our life.

How to Do It

A great deal has been written about gratitude writing and the psychological power of this form of writing for personal health, positive thinking and living. Yet it all boils down to a simple exercise:

- Writing a list of things you're grateful for is probably best done at the end of your day, before going to sleep.
- It's also good to have one special notebook by your bedside where you write your list.
- Aim to write three or five good things that happened that day for which you're grateful.
- The more specific the things you write about the better: sharing a joke with someone, having the door held open for you, a lovely walk at lunchtime in the park, a nice breakfast which you had time to enjoy, an unexpected phone call from an old friend, sitting on the sofa with your dog watching a great film.

Whether you decide to write three or five things, stick to that number or else go above it. That way you really zone in on remembering the good things that happened in your day. It is often only by doing this exercise that you remember things maybe from earlier in the day that you might have forgotten, or which might have been obliterated by what you consider to be a more negative event later. You then start to see that even on what you might consider a difficult or bad day you can easily spot some good things that also happened, which helps you to have a more balanced approach to adversity.

Reading Back Through Your Gratitude Journal

This is a helpful exercise when you hit the wall and think that the outlook is bleak.

Reading back through the pages of your gratitude journal provides concrete evidence, collected only by you, and over a sustained period, that good things happen to you every day. So the evidence in your gratitude journal can be savoured on days when you have managed to convince yourself that there is nothing good in your life or that you're a failure.

In addition to keeping a daily gratitude list, any of the following exercises are also useful to help foster a deep sense of appreciation in your life.

Gravy

Towards the end of his life, the wonderful writer Raymond Carver wrote a poem called 'Gravy' for what was to be his final anthology, *A New Path to the Waterfall*. He was dying of cancer but over the previous ten years he had changed from being a heavy drinker in danger of liver failure to being 'alive, sober, working'. He had also met 'a good woman' and was deeply in love. And so the poem, rather than bemoaning his untimely death at a time of great personal happiness, celebrates the second chance which he got at life – the gravy referred to in the title.

Try writing about what you consider to be the gravy in your own life: the unexpectedly good things that have happened to you, the stuff you did not see coming and yet which have immeasurably added to the richness of your life.

Present Blessings

'Reflect upon your present blessings – of which every man has many – not on your past misfortunes, of which all men have some' – Charles Dickens, 'A Christmas Dinner'.

Write about your present blessings. You might begin with a list and then write in more detail about one of these.

Letters of Gratitude

A study by Stephen Toepfer and Kathleen Walker in 2009 found that students who wrote three letters of gratitude to three different people over time were happier and more grateful in the weeks subsequently.

> Try drafting a letter of gratitude to someone in your life. Perhaps this is someone you're no longer in contact with or the person may be dead. Or if it's someone you still see you might consider sending this letter to them or reading it to them face to face.

In the Dark Wood

The following lines from Dante's *Inferno* describe how in the darkest of times, good things can unexpectedly emerge. In serious illness, we can find courage. When we feel we have lost the way, we might find sudden inspiration.

> Just halfway through this journey
> I found myself inside a dark wood
> The right road lost
> But I found goodness there
>
> – Dante's *Inferno*

> Write about the goodness you found in your own dark wood.

Capturing the Precious Moments

Cesar Kuriyama, the designer of the 1 Second Everyday app, quit his advertising job and started recording one second of his own life each day when he turned 30. Kuriyama said that the project helped him to get through the tough days, appreciate the good days and prevent all his days from blurring together.

Kuriyama argues that curating short video clips of your life can be very powerful: 'Recording a moment daily started encouraging me to wake up and seize each day.'

> Write a list of captured moments from the past week. From the list pick one and write about it in detail using all your senses; really try to capture the essence of what made this experience worth savouring. Try keeping a small pocket notebook to capture such moments or, maybe like Kuriyama, you might film a one-second moment in each day.

Haiku

A haiku is a Japanese poem structure with three lines using five, seven and then five syllables, making a total of seventeen syllables. Haiku is a wonderful structure to capture vivid sense memories. You can find plenty of examples on *Haiku-poetry.org*.

> Try capturing sense memories using haiku as a structure. You could, for example, do this every day for a week, which gives you a chance to play around with the structure, perhaps shortening a line here and there so that the poem is as succinct as it can be.

Magical Moments

When my father tore up the back of a used cigarette packet and a man with a hat suddenly appeared, or when a folded piece of paper became a flying aeroplane it seemed like magic to my four-year-old eyes.

Describe a time in your life when you watched the world with glittering eyes.

- What did you see or hear?
- Did you once hear the faint sound of reindeer bells on Christmas Eve?
- Did you wake one morning to see for the first time a strangely hushed white world with snowflakes drifting past your bedroom window?

Scenes

I once witnessed the most spectacular dawn in a house perched above the sea. It unfolded over perhaps half an hour, inky greys veering to soft pinks to deep gold. Because I immediately wrote about what I had witnessed, the memory is fresh and captured for me to keep.

Write about a view you love. This could be a view from a house you stayed in once but that has taken hold in your heart. It could be a view you see every day or a memory from a time long since passed. It could be a place captured at a particular time of the day, such as sunset or dawn.

What feelings and memories does this view evoke?

The Peace of Nature

Wendell Berry describes so beautifully the soothing powers of wild natural environments in his poem 'The Peace of Wild Things'.

- Describe a time in your life when you sought peace in the power of nature, perhaps walking on a beach or lying under a favourite tree.

- Describe the place and what it means to you now or meant to you then.
- Where do you now go to rest in 'the peace of wild things'?

Much Loved Places

My childhood summers were spent on my uncle's farm in Mayo. The house had been built by my uncles and I loved it. As an adult I can appreciate what was good about the building itself. Every room had light streaming through from large windows on two sides. There was a beautiful sense of proportion to the rooms. But to my childhood self all I knew was that I loved being there.

Write about a building that you love.

- Do you still go there?
- What does it mean to you?
- What memories does it hold?
- If this place had a voice, what would it say to you?

Lost Places

I once went to an art exhibition on a small island where we were staying on holidays. One of the most evocative paintings was of a small rundown shed with layers of old paint peeling off the wood. I recognised it immediately as a place beside the beach where I swam every day. The artist had captured the falling-down shed to reflect its great dignity and even beauty.

Look for abandoned places, old broken-down buildings you pass by every day: abandoned ghost estates, run-down, closed shops. These are the empty spaces between the things we normally pay attention to: the traffic, someone passing us by on the footpath, the shiny, shouty new buildings that call for us to admire them.

Empty spaces can be an opportunity to pay attention, to wake up to something new in our world.

- What do you think about when you see this place?
- Who once lived here?
- Who hoped to live here but never did?

Remembered Rooms

Saki's short story 'The Lumber Room' vividly describes a room and all that it contains from the point of view of a small boy called Nicholas, including a vividly conjured scene from an old tapestry which to him becomes 'a living breathing story'.

Describe a room you love:

- Imagine yourself entering this room.
- Wander around, pick up things lying around.
- Sit and savour what this means.
- Is there a cupboard or a place you want to explore?
- What do you find there?

Smells

One of the most powerful of our senses is the sense of smell, which evokes memories in us and transports us back to times in the past that were significant for us.

What are the evocative smells you remember?

- The smell of diesel in a garage you worked in?
- The smell of roses in a garden?
- Hospital food?
- Floor or furniture polish?
- French cigarettes?

What are the memories this smell evokes? Write about that time.

Write to Recall

Try keeping a diary not as an everyday record of what you do but rather as a vivid recollection of a specific time and place you want to remember, or a scrap of conversation you thought was interesting, or something you saw that affected you. This is what writers do: they trap memories through painstaking note-taking so that they have a store of sense memories to draw on in their writing. Here is a wonderful description of the place where he grew up in West Virginia by the incredible writer Breece D'J Pancake:

> I open the truck's door, step onto the brick side street. I look at Company Hill again, all sort of worn down and round. A long time ago it was real craggy and stood like an island in the Teays River. It took over a million years to make that smooth little hill, and I've looked all over it for trilobites. I think how it has always been there and always will be, at least for as long as it matters. The air is smoky with summertime. A bunch of starlings swim over me. I was born in this country and I have never very much wanted to leave.
>
> 'Trilobites' (2014).

Try writing about your own version of 'Company Hill': a place that means a lot to you, that is somehow etched into your heart.

The Inner Mentor

Derek Walcott's poem 'Love after Love' describes the experience of coming face to face with your own self, 'the stranger who has loved you all your life'.

We are all familiar with the cranky voice in our head which tells us we aren't good enough or which runs us down or makes us feel insecure. We are probably less familiar with the inner mentor, that wise inner being, 'the stranger who has loved you all your life'. So in this exercise take time to listen to what the inner mentor has to say to you.

Imagine going on a trek up a hill. You get to the top. There is a beautiful view all around. It is a very peaceful place. Here you meet a wise old wizard. You sit on a rock facing the wizard. You start to have a conversation. Now write what it is you talk about, using your own voice and the voice of the wizard.

4

DEVELOPING FLOW

Recently I listened to a documentary about rally-driving by people who drive as a weekend hobby, travelling around to different rallies. For the navigator, every rally involves learning a new course, with several stages, through a set of pace notes. The navigator reads the pace notes for each stage as the driver drives the course. In the documentary, one of the navigators describes what it feels like to do her job: 'There's an adrenalin rush. You're concentrating on what is in the notes. You're in the zone.' And the driver described what it feels like to drive a stage: 'a stage takes ten minutes and for those ten minutes, you're free. It's you, the road. You forget about everything. You think about nothing else. You're free. All you think about is the road.' These quotes describe a sense of flow, a total sense of engagement in a challenging task.

The Hungarian psychologist Mihaly Csikszentmihalyi describes how when we are deeply involved in trying to reach a goal or engaged in an activity that is challenging but well suited to our skills, when the outcome matters to us, our actions are effortless and our mindset changes from that of fear and avoidance to that of engagement and openness, and we experience a joyful state called 'flow'.

The conditions for flow states include:

- That you are clear on your goals and that you get immediate feedback on progress towards them. You know what you've got to achieve and you know exactly how well you are doing.
- The activity you are engaged in requires skill and is challenging.
- There is complete concentration on what you are doing at the present moment so that actions and awareness are merged. A guitar player, for example, merges with the instrument and becomes the music that he plays. The activity becomes almost automatic, and the involvement seems almost effortless.
- There is a loss of reflective self-consciousness – what is often referred to as being 'in the zone'.
- You maintain a sense of personal control: people in flow feel that they are in control of what they are doing. They are not worried about failing.
- There is a distortion of the experience of time. Time is experienced often as being faster than expected, though people in flow often also report that time seems to slow down.
- The activity is experienced as being intrinsically rewarding. You engage in this activity because it is rewarding in itself. You do it for the joy of doing it.

Why is flow important? Flow experiences are so strongly related to happiness because they help us become resilient during the hard times. That is what Mihaly Csikszentmihalyi first noticed in his experiences during the Second World War: that the people who were most resilient when their day-to-day life was upended by the war were those who could find joy and happiness in challenging activities that they had always enjoyed, like playing chess. If you can submerge into flow experiences on a regular basis then when you hit hard times you can always rely on flow experiences to steady you, to give you some sense of joyful freedom even if you feel confused or sad or angry.

Flow fosters creativity and divergent thinking. Working on challenging tasks helps us think outside the box and come up with innovative solutions to problems, either individually or in teams. The experience of flow is also about being fully engaged and immersed in the experience of the present moment. When we are in flow, we tend to lose sight of our internal critic. We are no longer self-consciously considering whether we are 'doing it right' but instead we lose ourselves in the task.

Anchoring Practices

Finding and Developing Flow Activities

You may already be aware from the description above of the activities in your life that give you a sense of flow. Maybe you're one of the lucky people who already has plenty of flow experiences in your life. You've already found things to do that give you a real sense of challenge and joy, that you do because they are intrinsically rewarding. Whether its knitting, playing music, windsurfing or football, you know already what makes you joyful.

The sense of flow that Mihaly Csikszentmihalyi has identified increases our performance, our sense of self-esteem and our ability to concentrate. Flow experiences are also highly correlated with happiness. So how do you identify experiences that provide a sense of flow?

What I Really Love to Do Is ...

Think about activities that you enjoy a lot, that require skill, and which are challenging enough to be rewarding. When you think about it, most skills are like that: cooking, driving, painting. The skill could be something to do with your work or a hobby you love, like climbing or dancing or baking. The key is to set aside some time when you can focus on developing this skill, setting yourself new challenges and goals so that this becomes a rewarding and regular experience in your life.

Lost Skills

If you can't think of any activity that you love to do and that is challenging, then think back to the kinds of things you loved to do when you were younger. When were you at your most creative in your life? Maybe you loved tinkering with cars, riding your bike, making things with your hands, skating, painting, swimming or hiking. There may be skills you have completely left aside that you once loved and practised regularly but as your life got busier you just forgot all about them. Describe two or three skills you have, things you like to do and are good at. The skills could be to do with your work or with hobbies like cooking or baking, or maintaining fitness – like being a seriously good backstroke swimmer or having a low golf handicap – or it could be something else entirely like singing opera or speed reading or effortlessly doing cryptic crosswords.

- Why did you learn this skill? Did someone teach you? What does it mean to you to be good at this?
- Do you dedicate time to this skill? Could you do more? What one step could you take to use this skill you love?

Work and Flow

Depending on the kind of role you have, you may get a sense of flow from the work that you do – when you feel fully engaged with a task, so immersed that time seems to speed up. Flow experiences in work can enhance our sense of ourselves as being strong and creative as well as providing us with a highly rewarding sense of achievement and satisfaction. Flow can help us feel more connected to our work and make it easier to put in extra effort when necessary without it feeling like a chore. Sometimes, if you're working at the top of your game on a project or a process, each new challenge becomes something you relish, a new opportunity to expand your skills.

There may be some activities in work that give you flow experiences but probably many other tasks that are more mundane. If you're lucky enough to find flow in your work, then try to foster it by setting time aside for the tasks that you find rewarding, that fully engage you. Try to get free of distractions and then allow yourself to submerge in the task itself.

There are probably aspects of your work that you don't enjoy. It could be most aspects if you don't like what you do. But over the course of your working life were there times when you were so absorbed in what you were doing that you lost track of time? When you really enjoyed the challenge? Is there anything in your present job that mirrors that experience?

It doesn't matter whether the work you do is manual or desk-based so long as there is an element of challenge and skill in what you do.

Now try to look for opportunities to rise to the challenge and build your skills. If you just can't see any potential for flow in your work could you work with a mentor or coach to help you seek out opportunities for flow experiences either in work or outside of it?

Baby Steps

If you already have some inkling of what you think you might like to try to get skilled at, then instead of waiting for the perfect moment and the right conditions why not try taking small, achievable steps right now? Goethe was right: begin it now! The perfect time will not come around. You probably know that already deep down.

And maybe there isn't one big thing you want to do or be, so experiment. Not everyone has one true calling. Maybe you have different skills and talents. Explore your passions by trying different things; it helps a lot to avoid the pressure of feeling like you have to find 'the one thing' you're good at. Over the course of our lives we might find ourselves working in different careers or taking up different pastimes, joining a choir then maybe leaving it behind. Instead of seeing changes like this as evidence that you never stick with things, you could see it as evidence that you're open to moving on and exploring new experiences.

Be Prepared to Put in Time Practicing

On an activity holiday in Croatia, my husband and I tried kayaking in a two-person kayak. There was perhaps some chance that either of us on our own might have picked up the basics, at least enough to negotiate our way around the bay we were in, but together we were a pure disaster. As kayaking was one of the key activities on the holiday, the organisers strongly encouraged us to keep going but after trying to paddle our way for a couple of hours we both gave up.

> Becoming skilled at anything takes time and flow experiences don't suddenly happen very early on when you try something new. The whole idea of flow is that you are fairly skilled at what you do and it gives you joy and positive feedback to engage in the activity, whether that's playing chess, writing code, composing music or indeed kayaking. And the only way you get skilled is to put in the hours practicing, and then one day you find that you've managed to ski down a slope without falling or kayaked around a tricky course without losing the paddle or having to stop to take a break. At the stage when the skill becomes something that feels pretty natural, then you might begin to feel that joy of doing something you have begun to love and doing it well.

Teams and Flow

Flow experiences are highly rewarding and enjoyable and can greatly enhance our experience of working in teams. Working as part of a team can enhance the opportunities for flow experiences through collaborative problem-solving and working towards the achievement of a common goal. What team experiences have you enjoyed in the past? Do you have any opportunities to work with a team on a specific project, either in work or as a volunteer in a community group? All team sports and other group activities like singing in a choir or playing in a band offer huge potential to become fully engaged in doing something that is enjoyable, absorbing and challenging.

> Think about possible teams or groups that you could get involved in now.

- Is there a new project in work that you might opt into?
- Is there a community group working on enhancing the physical environment where you live? A drama group looking for new members?

Simplify Your Life and Discover What You Want to Focus On

If you struggle to figure out what flow means to you, one way to get to the core activities that you love is to think about stripping back your life to the things that you really consider important. One of my favourite shows to watch on television is *Tiny House Nation*, a programme in which people decide to move to a tiny house, usually under 1,000 square feet. Of course to downsize to a much smaller living space means letting go of a lot of possessions. Most people find this process difficult at the beginning: deciding what is essential and what is not. It's interesting to watch the follow-up one month or so after they have moved to their tiny house. Not only do people get along fine without all the stuff they got rid of, but often they have even gotten rid of more stuff since they moved, and they generally describe feeling lighter and more liberated.

Paring down the amount of stuff in your life by decluttering your clothes, books, papers and other possessions can have a surprising effect on productivity and energy. The process may also help you figure out what it is you really treasure, and so you may begin to see opportunities to experience more of a sense of flow in your life by engaging in activities you really love to do.

Try reading a blog like *www.becomingminimalist.com* or *zenhabits.net* for ideas on the approach to living a simpler life.

Flow and the Practice of Free Writing

Csikszentmihalyi's factors of flow correspond well to the experience of free writing:

- Clear goals (in free writing you write for a set number of minutes without stopping)
- Intense and focused concentration on the present moment (the aim of free writing is to just dive in and write, without lifting your pen from the page)
- Merging of action and awareness (people who free write often describe 'getting lost' in the task)
- A loss of reflective self-consciousness (the aim of free writing is to lose awareness of our internal critic which comments and reflects on everything we write. The aim is simply to go with the flow of writing)
- A sense of personal control over the activity (free writing is a very good way of achieving a sense of confidence in your own ability to write because there are no expectations of what the result will be)
- A distortion of temporal experience (in writing groups it is very common for writers to be surprised when the time is up)
- Experience of the activity as intrinsically rewarding (free writing has no end goal. In a writing group we never read this writing to others. The writing itself can be binned or never read back even by the person who wrote it. The aim of free writing is simply to write)

You dive in, pen in hand, and ten minutes later you emerge from the deep pool of your unconscious. Free writing can and often does catch people off guard. You may come to the table sure that you won't be able to concentrate, too caught up in the events and pressures of the day. But there is something about the experience of just letting go, of following the simple instructions to keep writing and not think about it that catches you off guard and gives permission to do just that.

What Is Free Writing?

Free writing is when you write for a short and specific amount of time without stopping, and without thinking about what you write – this part is key. You must park that narky internal critic who likes to tell you that you're a rubbish writer. When people join an expressive writing group, they often preface their participation by saying they are 'a poor writer'; for many of us there is a legacy with writing that runs very deep. This legacy can stop us in our tracks; we have internalised that fear in the form of a strong internal critic who voices that fear: 'this is stupid', 'this makes no sense'.

So how do you get over this fear? Free writing is a journey into the unknown. In a sense it's like walking the Camino: others have trodden the path, but the journey is never the same. There are no preconceptions of what the end product will be.

In free writing, there is permission to not hold back, to just dive in and see what happens. It is like play, just mooching about with a pen and paper, no agenda in mind. But what can be found are jewels of insights in the writing as we make sense of and sieve through our thoughts and feelings. Free writing is, therefore, a wonderful prequel to further writing exercises, much in the way that stretching exercises are essential for runners or ballet dancers to limber up before more strenuous exercise.

Imagine yourself writing with magic earplugs in your ears that not only shut out the noise around you but also the noise in your head – that high-pitched quarrelsome voice that says you can't write. As you write in this way, your confidence quickly grows, and it becomes easier to ignore the internal critic.

A key aspect of free writing is the idea of having a fixed time for the exercise. The idea that there is a definite end point and that either a timer or phone alarm or the writing facilitator will call time gives people permission to just go for it. It's not an open-ended exercise. There is a definite end in sight.

If you get stuck, just write about that. You can keep writing the same words over and over until eventually you will probably find that something loosens up and off you go taking another slant or tack. So, if you get stuck, don't be afraid of writing about what it's like to be stuck, not to be able to think of anything.

Free Writing as Meditation

Writing can have similar effects on the brain as meditation. Your breathing slows down and you can get into a zone where words flow freely. Stream-of-consciousness writing can be a very effective way of relaxing and lowering stress levels. Buster Benson makes the argument that writing is like meditation because there is a specific limitation of time; there is the gentle persistence of staying on track during that time by continuing to write, of being an observer of your writing as opposed to a critic. All the ideas and words in your head flow onto the page and you just watch the process without interfering in it or analysing or censoring what is written. You, as writer, stay out of the process and let the writing hand do its work. Benson, a writer/researcher on free writing, and a blogger at *750words.com*, argues that the act of writing or typing is akin to doing the dishes or gardening. It allows the brain to just wander or, as he puts it, like hitching your subconscious to your fingers. He points out that in meditation you can easily get side-tracked by thoughts that bubble to the surface whereas in free writing you are so busy writing that you are unlikely to get distracted by your own writing ideas because you are still busy continuously writing.

Free writing helps you be a mindful writer who is just writing and not thinking about what you are writing. There is a difference! This kind of writing is a different form of meditation which is very soothing and therapeutic. And what is more, this can sometimes lead you to your very best ideas. This type of writing cultivates flow – being fully engaged with a challenging task – and it is strongly connected to happiness.

Why Do It?

There are many benefits to free writing:

- Free writing forces you to be present in the moment. So much of our lives now is about reacting to what is happening through Twitter or Instagram or other social media platforms. A lot of our communication is in short, truncated messages of tweets, texts and emails. Unlike these platforms, free writing is all about you and the empty page. Free writing allows a dance between pen and paper where you can just go for it. It's a form of deep dive writing as opposed to swimming around on the surface.
- It allows you to free yourself for other writing by hoovering out all the thoughts floating around your head. In all the groups I have worked with, I always begin with some free writing, usually for ten minutes. This

gets us all in the zone to do other writing exercises. It really helps to clear out all the busy whirring thoughts that are 'monkey mind' – that is, thoughts that are unsettled, restless and uncontrollable – and, instead, to develop a sense of focus.

- When you come to sit down to write, you have so many things floating around in your head. 'What time is that appointment at tomorrow?', 'Do I need to put diesel in the car?', 'Should I have bought that dress I put on hold?' Free writing cuts through all that hum of busy thoughts. You might find yourself writing down all the above thoughts and more but, after a few minutes, you might also find yourself beginning to write about other things: 'Why do I always put clothes I'm buying on hold? Why do I not make the decision on the spot? I'm always dithering about everything. Why is that?' You get to a place where you express with clarity something that rings true, that strikes you as making sense, some truth that you know in your heart is valuable. Free writing is about writing down the bones, as author on writing and the doyen of free writing Natalie Goldberg says: getting to the heart of what it is you really want to express.

- Free writing lets your imagination go wild. It's like taking a walk through your thoughts and ideas. But it's more like a ramble. You're not in any hurry here. Okay, there is that timer that will go off but, inside the free write itself, there is time to examine an idea, then drop it and go on to explore another path and sometimes, gloriously, you find that two paths join up in the end. Ideas that seemed to just drop onto the page for no reason suddenly and meaningfully connect with other ideas. Because free writing is all about tapping into the unconscious mind, the real benefit is just that: that we

connect things we might never have connected if we
didn't take a ramble and start rummaging through all
these disparate ideas and feeling and thoughts.

- Free writing is beneficial for generating ideas for a
  book, an essay, a report, a poem, or anything you like.
  It is brainstorming for writers which gets you over the
  'I've nothing to write about', chewing-your-pen phase.
  The blank page is a menacing thing and full of terror
  for most people. But having a timer and a set of simple
  instructions to just write about anything somehow
  gives people permission to just dive in and begin.
- Free writing allows you to forget yourself in writing and
  just write. This is the Holy Grail for writers: to let go of
  that infernal internal critic whose nasty whiny voice
  tells them that everything they are writing is drivel.
  Free writing muffles that voice. It is so much easier
  to just write when you haven't set up the expectation
  that you are writing 'my new novel' or 'my short story'.
  Instead you're just tearing through the pages with a
  simple free write but you might be very surprised at
  what comes out of the exercise.
- Free writing can help you to explore an issue in depth,
  to submerge yourself in a topic in a concentrated way. If
  you've got a challenging task ahead – a writing assignment for college, a speech to write, a presentation to
  prepare – free writing can be a wonderful way to start.

How to Do It

Try to pick a time when you won't be disturbed. What you
are aiming for is deep dive writing. Just like it's danger-
ous for divers to surface too quickly, free writing hopefully
gets you into a meditative place where you're no longer
consciously self-critical about what you write. Instead you

are at one with the pen, the paper and the words. So any interruptions, such as someone popping their head around the door asking if you have seen the car keys, will make you surface out of this meditative state too quickly in a way that makes it unlikely that you will be able to quickly regain that level of being lost in what you are writing again.

In picking a time to free write you might like to choose early in the morning. The writer Dorothea Brande advocated writing as soon as you wake up, to capture that dreamy state. The big advantage of early morning is that you may be less likely to be disturbed, but really it's whatever works for you. If you manage to establish a comfortable morning routine then that is wonderful. If, on the other hand, you free write only now and then and never manage to pin down a specific time of the day, then so be it. It really is a question of whatever works best for you. There are simply no hard and fast rules. There are advocates of free writing who insist that it should be done faithfully every day, but I am not one of them.

Free writing is a useful writing tool in all the ways I have already described, and I turn to it at all sorts of times in my life, having found it to be a consistently useful tool within writing groups and for myself.

Writing Longhand or Typing?

If you feel more comfortable writing longhand with pen and paper, then do that. If you're a whizz at typing your thoughts – and many people do type much faster than they write – then type your free writes on to a blank screen. The website *750words.com*, mentioned in the resource list, might be perfect for you. You can always delete the whole thing if you don't want to save it. However, writing longhand is very soothing and the change to writing by hand can also be a quiet signal to your imagination that this is play time and anything goes.

***

I hope most of all that you get to experience the sheer exhilaration of free writing. How a space opens up in which you can spill everything onto an empty page: the rage you felt when your friend was late yesterday; the boredom of all the work you're facing into today; concerns about the family such as wondering if your mother is really okay because she didn't sound too good on the phone; wondering if you should consider doing an educational course and change the direction of your life; and on and on till your buzzing thoughts unravel. Thoughts, images, feelings fall gently through the sieve when you free write and, in my experience of hundreds, probably thousands, of my own free writes, what often happens is that I reach some conclusion – things add up or my writing leads me in a wholly unexpected direction. It's like you get to the nub of the issue. Okay, so you began writing about how fed up you are with one of your kids not doing anything around the house and you find yourself remembering how you felt the day of their birth and then you write about how bereft you are that they will be leaving home soon and what are you going to do then? That's it you see: free writing can take you anywhere.

So now that you know what free writing is about, in the following pages I explain the basic practice of how to do free writing and give you some other exercises as variations on the basic practice which you might like to try out. The resource list provides information on the topic from seasoned practitioners in the field of free writing that you may also wish to explore.

The Basic Practice of Free Writing

There are a number of activities that assist us in the basic practice of free writing:

- Set a timer on your phone for ten minutes (or five if you like, though ten is better).
- Write; preferably without stopping.
- Write about anything you want and if you can't think of anything to write about just write the sentence 'I can't think of anything to write about ...' over and over until words begin to flow again.
- Don't worry at all about grammar, spelling or sentence structure. Nobody, not even you, needs to read what you have written. When you have finished writing you can, if you wish, bin your writing or burn it, or you can keep it if you want to do that. The choices are yours when you write. You can choose to read what you have written back to yourself or not. The key thing is that you do not stop to correct anything. Just go with the flow.
- Don't criticise. Don't stop to criticise or think about or analyse what you're writing about. Keep writing. Just imagine you're a diver on a boat and you've been given the signal to dive: so dive!

Writing on Set Topics

If you are going to write on a particular topic it can be helpful to set a timer and pick a specific topic such as:

- A tough decision you've been avoiding
- An idea you've been mulling over for a while
- An issue in your life you've been trying to figure out
- A conflict that seems intractable

Writing the Now

Sometimes our life is so busy that we become adrift from how we are, how we feel. In this exercise we drop back down into ourselves and ponder how we are. This helps to heighten your awareness of how you are feeling and how to achieve a greater sense of perspective on those feelings. For example, the following topics might be helpful:

- Right now, if I were a colour I would be ...
- What time of day would I be and why?
- If I were a flower, I would be ...
- If I were an animal, I would be ...
- If I were a car, I would be ...
- If I were a piece of furniture, I would be ...

The aim of the exercise is to quickly finish each of the above sentences and then pick the one that jumps out at you as being most resonant in terms of how you feel; the sentence that most accurately reflects your current state of mind. Then you might like to pick that sentence and elaborate. Build on that first sentence and write a little more.

Wild Writing

Write the name of a topic at the top of the page and then write without any attempt to order your thoughts. There are any number of topics from which you might choose.

For example, it could be an issue you've been struggling with at work, or a problem in your relationship with a friend, or it could be a tricky essay, a short story you've been trying to begin, a presentation you've been avoiding. Try writing wild. Don't censor your ideas. Let your imagination take over so you are no longer writing what you think is expected, what you *should* write.

This type of writing is fertile ground for you to explore avenues you might not have considered. At a later stage you can trawl through what you've written to sort out the useful from the not so useful. But right now, just write.

You could try several timed sessions on the same topic and then read back through what you have written. Underline words or phrases that ring true. Pick out any themes that keep repeating. Wild writing captures the kernel of your own ideas from the depths of your unconscious. It's authentic and, while it might seem jumbled, you will probably find some jewels in your trawl-through which will provide a stimulus for further writing.

Write to Music

Linda Trichter Metcalf, the founder of proprioceptive writing with her colleague Tobin Simon, recommends writing to the background sound of baroque music. Stephen King famously wrote his first novel sitting on top of the washing machine in his house. Who knows, maybe the drone of that drum going around and round was just the thing that inspired him?

Try experimenting with writing to a favourite piece of music.

Writing from Sentence Stems

Free writing is a way of coming to know ourselves, but there is a danger that we can write ourselves into a corner or a cul-de-sac. So we write about our grief or our sense of profound loss about someone or we write about our anger, and the pages fill up and read like one long rant against the world. If you read back through your writing, you will be able to find fairly quickly whether or not this is something that you do.

But is this helpful? Is writing a rant a helpful exercise? Not necessarily. What works best in this kind of writing is when people write to gain some clarity or insight into their feelings or thoughts. When the writing is a journey towards self-meaning; when writing helps us clarify an issue.

The best way to approach writing is to embark on a journey of self-discovery with the aim of getting somewhere else, to a place where we feel that we understand ourselves a little better, where we realise why we did what we did or why something upset us. Our writing helps to bring meaning where before there was a jumble of mixed-up emotions and thoughts, when it not only helps us express but also to clarify, to make meaningful, to understand.

Writing from sentence stems – unfinished sentences or cues which we then complete by writing from them – can be a helpful way of bringing more clarity into your writing. Using these sentence stems is especially helpful if you find your writing is going around in an endless loop without really going anywhere. The following exercise will give you an idea of how to use these sentence stems in a beneficial way.

Pick any one of the following sentence stems; in my experience one of them will always jump out at you, so pick the one that immediately resonates with you and just write. You can always come back and pick another one for another free write:

- This all happened because ...
- Now I realise ...
- It all fell into place when ...
- I have found that ...
- I see now that ...
- Now I understand ...

Sounds

Writing about and describing sounds is always useful. Write about a favourite sound: the wind through the trees, sea sounds, a baby laughing, the rumble of jets flying far above.

Think Like a Child

Look at the sense of wonder in small children, how they look at the world. Thinking like a child can bring us into imaginative spaces that facilitate our writing. If you can see your own world the way a child would see it what would it look like? Think about the larger-than-life images and metaphors that children's stories are soaked in, such as castles, princes, forests, treasure, wicked witches, long journeys and magical carpets. Write about an event in your life as a fairy story and use any or all of the metaphors here or bring in even more. Just let yourself fall into the writing of this story and free your imagination to go wild. Begin in a dark forest or take a trip on a magic carpet or look out at your kingdom from the turrets of your castle. I have done this exercise dozens of times myself and with groups and never found that it was awkward or difficult to do. We all remember the magical stories of our childhood.

> Go ahead and write your own version now, beginning with the immortal line: 'Once upon a time ....'.

Trawling Through

> Another useful writing exercise is trawling through what you have written previously. You could read back what you have written in a previous free writing session, underline any words or phrases that stand out to you and then pick one of these and start writing again.

Write from a Word

> Grab the nearest book or newspaper or magazine. Pick the first word on the page you open and start writing. This is often exactly what we need to fire the imagination: having your options narrowed to one word can open whole new vistas once you get started.

Write When You First Wake Up

> Capture your thoughts in that dreamy state between sleep and being fully awake.

Write and Draw Your Story

> Fill the page with doodles to match the words on the page, or drawings of a house you love or a garden or a map of a trip you once took.

Write in Your Favourite Genre

If you're a huge fan of fantasy fiction or crime writing, for example, try writing in that genre.

Forty-Nine Other Suggested Topics

And finally, here are 49 other ideas to free write:

- Write about your biggest fears
- Write about your gifts
- Write about friendships
- Write about the best thing you ever did
- Write you as hero
- Write you as searcher
- Write you as dreamer
- Write you in heaven
- Write you in hell
- Write you as perfect
- Write you as a mess
- Write you as starting out
- Write you as finishing up
- Write you as immersed in the middle
- Write you in the loop/in the know
- Write you in the cold/on the outside
- Write you as beautiful
- Write you as family
- Write about what was lost
- Write about what was found
- Write about what was forgotten
- Write about what was remembered
- Write about the loneliest time
- Write about the best time
- Write about honouring the dead

- Write about loving the living
- Write about saying goodbye
- Write about saying hello
- Write about unfamiliar places/travelling
- Write about opening up
- Write about closing down
- Write about fishing
- Write about birdsong
- Write about what is carried
- What about what is put down
- Write about how you sleep
- Write about losing perspective
- Write about gaining perspective
- Write about sunshine
- Write about long days
- Write about darkness
- Write about open space
- Write about childhood games
- Write about lost sounds
- Write about a gentle touch
- Write about ecstasy
- Write about boundless love
- Write about possibilities
- Write about choice

After You Write

It can be very useful to do this exercise at the end of a writing session, whether that is a free writing session or indeed any of the exercises in the chapters which follow. Reflecting on your writing through a further write can help you to become more mindfully aware of the effects of your writing. So, for example, you might reflect on the effects on you of writing:

- Did your breathing change as you wrote?
- Do you feel more relaxed or more tense as a result?
- Does your writing make sense?
- What have you learned about yourself? Do you want to write more on this topic?

The reflection might begin by writing from a sentence stem such as:

- Rereading this I see that ...
- Writing this I felt ...

5

THINKING FLEXIBLY: MOVING BEYOND
A ONE-STORY LIFE

In 1975, Denis Mulcahy, an NYPD bomb squad expert and an Irish emigrant, began a visionary scheme offering children from both sides of the political and religious divide in Northern Ireland a chance to take a break from the day-to-day violence of Northern Ireland and spend six weeks of their summer holidays with host families in New York and New Jersey. He saw it as an opportunity to keep children safe for a little while, perhaps to save some lives. From that first summer the project grew, extending to other cities over a 40-year period; 23,000 children from Northern Ireland took part.

Growing up in Northern Ireland at the height of the Troubles, Catholic and Protestant children would never have had the opportunity to meet. In Project Children they were often living together with the same host family. Some formed deep and, in some cases, life-long friendships and realised that they had much more in common than their differences. Through participating in the project the children were given the opportunity to be part of a wider story than the narrow confines of the sectarian divides of Northern Ireland during the Troubles. In the words of one of the participants, 'The experience with Project Children let me see a world beyond The Troubles; that there was a world outside Belfast and that has made all the difference in the world to me.'

Denis Mulcahy has been twice nominated for the Nobel Peace Prize and is widely credited as being highly influential in laying the groundwork for the peace process in Northern Ireland. He remains involved in this work to the present day.

We can all have a story that defines our lives. It all works well if the story you tell yourself is a positive one. I recently saw a Ted Talk from a 22-year-old college student with a full and wonderful life who suddenly became paraplegic, but he told a story about learning to ride a bike without stabilisers in one weekend when he was very young. Even though he fell down a lot, he persisted and rode his bike to school on the Monday morning. The story that he had internalised from this experience was that if you want something badly enough, then go for it, even if at first you fail. Just keep going. Be fearless. When he broke his neck in an accident many years later, he adopted the same attitude then: if you want to get through this then it's going to be hard but just keep going.

But what if the life-defining story is a negative one? If you listen to other people you can pick up the clues to their own story and often that story may be negative:

- 'If I hadn't failed my exams that time, I'd have finished college and I wouldn't be stuck for the rest of my life in this crumby job. I've lost my chance.'

- 'My father was a very angry man and I have real anger issues as a result; that's why I can't make any relationship work.'
- 'My parents doted on my sister and I never got any praise for anything I ever achieved.'

The problem with a negative story is that we get stuck in the story and it's the frame through which we judge everything that happens to us. When we are trapped with a one-story version of our life – such as 'I'll never amount to anything. I'm a failure at everything' – then shaking up your perspective helps you to see that you can change. It's possible to turn your story from negative to positive by altering perspective. Developing the ability to be flexible helps us to be more objective, and frees us from old ways of thinking and acting. Being flexible makes us more tolerant of change, of coping with new circumstances. It gives us a feeling that we can manage, that we can figure things out. We can stand back and see things more objectively and not feel overwhelmed by what is happening.

Getting beyond a one-story life is recognising that a negative story may be trapping you, explaining away why you're right and everyone else is wrong, why nobody else understands you, why you can't do anything to change the way things are, why life sucks.

Getting beyond a one-story life is about seeing the possibility of different scripts about your life, about reviewing life-defining events, good and bad, especially the ones which are central to how you see yourself. It's about broadening your perspective on your story and seeing it from other viewpoints.

In his book *The Shark and the Albatross: Travels with a Camera to the Ends of the Earth*, wildlife photographer John Aitchison describes filming the first flight of an albatross as it took off from a small island west of Hawaii. In fact, there were two film crews. Aitchison filmed the bird from a small cage just above the ocean while underwater divers filmed the predatory sharks lying in wait. The bird took flight but then came down to rest on the sea. A shark took its opportunity and soared out of the sea, mouth open. The frantic young albatross literally ran on the water, spreading its wings to take off again and succeeded. John Aitchison describes how, after filming the escape of the albatross, he inevitably sympathised with the bird, but the divers were full of admiration for the sharks: 'They spoke of the sharks' exquisite sense of timing and their extraordinary navigational skills which every year bring them to this tiny speck of land just as the first birds begin to fly. They pointed out that sharks are vital to the health of the ocean and in hushed tones describe their beauty and their shocking decline due to overfishing.' What is interesting in the account of the shark and the albatross is that the filmmakers' perspectives were influenced by the viewpoint from which they filmed the encounter.

Anchoring Practices

Becoming a Tourist in Your Own Life

The psychologist Ellen Langer talks about the importance of living with full attention and not mindlessly. Paying attention is about being open to noticing new things, even in situations which seem so familiar to us that we feel we already know them completely. We tend to operate on automatic pilot, using assumptions that have served us well so far, whether it's about people or our environment or our way of doing things.

So, for example, I enjoy sea swimming and swim at a local beach, usually at high tide. It's a big wide beach which is beside another, smaller one I had always assumed to be too rocky for swimming. I thought I knew this smaller beach well and didn't relish the idea of cutting myself on jagged rocks. What works for us is what we tend to repeat over and over, so I wasn't enthusiastic when a swimming friend suggested we try it, but my assumptions proved to be all wrong.

The rocks in fact form a natural outdoor swimming pool at low tide which is beautiful to swim in. The combination of my friend's enthusiasm and happening to go there at low instead of high tide helped me discover a wonderful natural pool. Being alert to new possibilities might help us discover, for example, lots of good places to swim. In fact, recently on my 'new' beach I met someone who is in the process of writing a book about all the best beaches, rivers and lakes to swim in Ireland, documenting the myriad of possibilities open to us to enjoy.

The Scottish artist and sculptor David Mach uses everyday objects like pins and matches, tyres and newspapers to create works of extraordinary beauty and breath-taking imagination. His wide-ranging and very impressive catalogue of work ranges from small sculptural works of beauty such as colourful patterned vases made from pins to large installations featuring cars, caravans and even boats. Colourful sweet papers become beautiful figures. He describes how he uses matches and coat hangers to create his sculptures: 'I get very excited by material and what I can do with it.' What is to most people a functional everyday object is to him something of potential to be transformed into anything, the only limits set by his own imagination.

One way to begin to widen your own perspective is to practice being more open to new experiences. In our day-to-day encounters, we usually filter everything we see and experience through the kinds of prejudices and beliefs we have cultivated from being immersed in the culture we live in. When we travel to other countries, we are usually wide awake and downright curious and so much more open to new experiences. We talk of soaking up the culture with the wide-eyed curiosity and wonder of a child. From the moment the plane lands, we are switched on; we point things out to each other. In a new place we pay attention: what's this place like? What are the good things about it that we like? What is beautiful? What is worth taking a photo of? What happened here? What is its history? What are the people like? What does the food taste like?

As we notice all these new things, we are engaged, wide awake and interested in everything new. Our mindset tends to be very open because we don't know what to expect. But once we get back home, we take everything for granted again because it's all so familiar and we fall back into construing our world through our own well-worn beliefs. We know what to expect and because it's all so familiar we can operate pretty effortlessly on automatic pilot. It's what we do all the time, isn't it? We take things for granted. We run through the familiar rabbit runs of our lives and don't stop to smell the coffee. Savouring the sweetness of the simple things in life is not easy to maintain. We get busy and we take it all for granted again.

But what if you tried from time to time to adopt that same sense of openness, that wide-eyed curiosity about others that we have when we travel? How much more could you learn if your eyes and ears were really open to new experiences? You might have more chance encounters with people; you might suddenly notice a lovely building you pass every day on your commute to work.

So become a tourist in your own life. Being a tourist in your own life is about approaching each day with a renewed sense of wonder and, in doing so, widening your view of the world you live in by being curious and open to new experiences. It's about adopting an attitude of wide-eyed childlike wonder, even for a small time during your day. It is also about being mindful because mindfulness is about fully engaging with the present moment and being wide awake to the changing flow of experience right here, right now.

The Ten-Minute Focus

We can adopt a wide-eyed curiosity of places that are familiar to us. We can wake up from being on automatic pilot to being open to new experiences. Try walking through your world with your eyes wide open.

Decide that for ten minutes today you are really going to wake up and pay attention with real focus on something or someone. It might be for the time you're on the bus or in the car commuting to work. Just notice what you see on the journey: clouds scudding across the sky, an old building you never noticed before. Or it could be a time when you're meeting a friend for coffee. Instead of being half-switched off, try for ten minutes to focus with all the attention you can muster. Imagine your friend is someone you have met on a train or a bus and listen intently with a wide sense of curiosity. Or take a walk with your eyes wide open. Be curious, learn something new. Challenge, change and learning are really good for your brain health as well as helping you to appreciate more of this wonderful world which Louis Armstrong sang about.

Notice Small Details

In *Zen and the Art of Motorcycle Maintenance*, the main protagonist, who calls his alter ego Phaedrus, describes a scene in which Phaedrus, a college lecturer, tries to help a student with a writing assignment on the United States of America. She can't think of anything to say so he suggests that she write instead about Bozeman, the town where the college is located. But she is still stumped. Write about the main street, he suggests. Still nothing. Frustrated, he finally suggests she writes about a building there, the opera house, but that she should write just about the brick in the top left-hand corner.

He describes what happens next. 'She came in the next class with a puzzled look and handed him a five-thousand-word essay on the front of the opera house on the main street of Bozeman, Montana. "I sat in the hamburger joint across the street," she said, "and started writing about the first brick, and then the second brick, and then by the third brick it all started to come and I couldn't stop."'

> Try this: slow down and notice the small things that happen in your day. Take a notebook or use the camera on your phone to capture a small moment, a brick in a building, a hole in the footpath or a horse in a field. Doing so will sharpen your antennae to see the world in more detail, to notice the richness and the beauty of everyday objects and events.

Deeply Listening

Think about a time in your life when someone deeply listened to you. Maybe a teacher really paid attention and listened to what you had to say. Maybe a friend spent time with you when you were going through a rough time. Maybe you went to a great therapist.

- What did this experience mean to you?
- How did it change you?
- What was it like?

When was the last time someone listened to you with full attention? When did you notice this and how did it make you feel? Listening wholeheartedly to someone is a real and perhaps rare gift as we get so distracted by technology and social media. Listening in this way means setting aside our preconceptions about what we think the person will say, not second-guessing them.

Nelson Mandela knew that as President of South Africa he had to build bridges between the black majority and the white minority. He used rugby as one way to do that and, specifically, through the staging of the Rugby World Cup in his country. As the Springboks team had been a central plank of apartheid, with many other teams refusing to play them, the sport of rugby was a very potent symbol to white South Africans. In convincing the new government to go along with his idea he said:

I believe we should restore the Springboks, restore their name, their emblem and their colours. Let me tell you why. On Robben Island, in Pollsmoor Prison, all of my jailers were Afrikaners. For 27 years, I studied them. I learned their language, read their books, their poetry. I had to know my enemy before I could prevail against him. Our enemy is no longer the Afrikaner. They are our fellow South Africans, our partners in democracy. And they treasure Springbok rugby. If we take that away, we lose them. We prove that we are what they feared we would be. We have to be better than that. We have to surprise them with compassion, with restraint and generosity.

Focus more on listening deeply to someone when you have a conversation with them. You might even get to change your mind about them or at least learn something new. You might have coffee or lunch with somebody at work you used to think of as being aloof, a bit snooty. You might discover something amazing, like that he loves writing crime fiction and the reason he doesn't often go to the canteen for lunch is that he uses that as his writing time. Who knew!

Developing Tolerance

You might have noticed sometimes when you attend a funeral people will say, 'she never had a bad word to say about anyone.' Wouldn't that be a wonderful eulogy? To be seen as a tolerant, kind person who wasn't known for 'bad-mouthing' others? It's interesting that this trait of not gossiping is so often seen as a noble trait, a key way in which we sum up someone's life.

Conversations where we give full vent to our opinions on someone else is something most of us do without even being conscious that we're doing it, and it's a one-way street in which we reinforce each other's views in a negative way about someone who isn't there to defend themselves. If this is something you sometimes do, you could decide to give up talking negatively about other people, enabling you to have more productive conversations as well as freeing you from falling into negative spirals in relation to other people.

Shake Up Your View of the World

Try shaking up your view of the way things should be by bringing new experiences into your life. Maybe try reading a newspaper you don't normally read or watching a documentary on a topic that you know nothing about. Get to see things from the other side. Take a new route home. Order something completely different next time you eat out or get takeaway.

Conscious Compassion

You could consciously decide to practice being more compassionate in your relationships. Compassion is about being able to feel for other people. We talk about standing in someone else's shoes.

One way to foster a sense of compassion is to use a guided meditation to develop a deep empathy for people we know, especially when we struggle in our relationship with them. On her website, clinical psychologist and meditation teacher Tara Brach provides many different guided meditations; one in particular is useful to try in relation to stepping into someone else's shoes, which is the theme of this chapter. It's called 'The RAIN of Compassion' and it is quite a long guided meditation but towards the end it contains an exercise in stepping into someone else's shoes (you choose whose shoes) and experiencing the world from their viewpoint. It is a very powerful exercise in feeling a real sense of compassion for another person, especially if you are finding it difficult, if the relationship you have with this person is stuck in some way. You can find a link to the exercise itself on Tara's website: *www.tarabrach.com/rain-of-compassion*.

Blue and Green Exercise

Green spaces give us an opportunity to see the bigger picture in our lives, to reflect on our goals, where we are and where we want to go. For example, wilderness experiences have been used for adolescents with behavioural or self-esteem issues to foster reflection over week-long expeditions, with improvements frequently reported, such as a growth in self-esteem, self-confidence, self-empowerment and decision-making. In studies of outdoor pre-schools, where children play outside in all weathers, children with so-called 'challenging' behaviour seem much happier and better behaved because the environment is freer and fosters highly imaginative play, allowing them to release pent-up energy as well as working in teams to get things done like chopping wood or helping to build a camp fire.

I've spent the past summer, like many others, swimming in the waters around our coast. I know that even on days when there is a bit of wind or rain that has sent the beach walkers scattering back to their cars, I invariably emerge from the waves wearing a silly grin. I know this because I've witnessed the same expression so many times on other swimmers' faces. There is something truly magical about wild swimming and the benefits are now the subject of research.

Psychology has recently focused much more on the mental health benefits of green and blue therapy, in other words being in nature near forests, parks and woodland or near lakes, beaches or rivers. Anecdotally, people who swim all year round point out that immersing yourself in cold water leaves little room for negative thinking. You just have to be in the moment.

Think about getting some blue or green exercise. There are very real benefits to getting out in nature for some exercise, not the least of which is it can help give us a new perspective on difficult issues. There's nothing like a walk on a beach or a run through the woods to help us to see our problems in the greater scheme of things, helping us to see the big picture.

Writing and Flexible Thinking

James Pennebaker's research has shown that people who change pronoun use in their writing tend to achieve better health outcomes as a result. In his original writing experiment, people were asked to write for three or four consecutive days on the most traumatic experience of their lives. What Pennebaker and his researchers noticed was that some writers began their writing using the pronoun 'I' but within a day or so had begun to use other perspectives such as 'she' or 'he'. So, what these writers were doing was standing back and considering the bigger picture rather than staying wholly absorbed in their own version of events. This widening of perspective and ability to switch viewpoints helped them to make sense of the story they were telling.

Why do it?

- You become a more flexible thinker. This type of writing widens the lens through which you look at past events. It gives you a broader picture. Obviously if you write from someone else's perspective it is still you writing but you're saying to yourself, 'what if I look at this from this person's viewpoint? What will I learn from that? How would they see it differently?'
- You begin to see that there is more than one version of events. If it's a conflict you're writing about, you begin to see that maybe the other person had some valid

points to make or that things looked different from their side.

- You develop a deeper and richer understanding of the issue you write about.
- You have an opportunity to meet your inner mentor. We all have a strong internal critic who is always ready to pounce and criticise everything we do. Writing about our emotions, for example, can help us see that we are bigger than any of our feelings. We can be kind to ourselves and not feel so overwhelmed by anger or anxiety or self-blame.
- For writers who want to write fiction, it gives you endless possibilities for widening the lens of your story or fleshing out your characters with a lot more depth.
- When you write in someone else's voice you use their language, their expressions. This gives you a different slant, a different mindset.
- When you write using metaphor you can see the issue in a more objective way so that you can create more distance between you and the events you are writing about. This helps you to make sense of the experience which, up to now, may have seemed so overwhelming that you tried to push it away. Making sense of our experiences allows us to let go of the emotions surrounding it. The story loses its power.

How to Do It

Before you start it might help to think about your life to date. What are the key events, the stand-out moments, good and bad? You might like to make a list of the momentous events in your life. While these milestone events might be things like getting married and the birth of your children, the list could also include things like breaking up with your first love or the day the teacher ridiculed you in front of the whole class; in other words, moments that you see as pivotal, that you remember vividly. Pick a moment from your list that jumps out at you. Probably something will.

The following exercises are designed to shake up your view, to encourage you to adopt new ways of looking at these events. When we write about events which we consider to be pivotal moments in our lives, we can dredge up painful memories. As I have already mentioned, research has shown that people who write about very negative experiences may initially feel worse because of the intense recall of events that are painful. Usually having the opportunity to write about that experience in depth helps them to integrate and make sense of the experience. In the following exercises, whatever perspective you decide to take, take care of yourself. As I already mentioned in the introduction, if writing becomes a deeply upsetting experience for you, simply stop. Or share what you've written with a friend or perhaps a therapist.

Being Flexible

In the Irish language there is an old saying (seanfhocail) – 'Is fearr lúbadh na briseadh' – which means 'Better to bend than break'. The saying refers to times in our lives when we are tempted to hold our ground, even if it may mean being stubborn or pig-headed instead of being willing to bend in our opinion, to reach out for a joint solution, to compromise.

- Describe a time in your life when you were willing to bend or describe a time when you did not bend but you wished you had.

- Or write about someone you know, perhaps someone in your family, who held to their own opinion and refused to bend at all. What was the result? How did things turn out?

Toy Story

There's a heartrending scene in *Winnie the Pooh* when Christopher Robin has to say goodbye to Pooh, his much-loved toy bear, before he heads off into the new world of boarding school. Pooh has been his companion on so many of his adventures but alas not on this one.

Your favourite toy may have been the neutral observer of your childhood. If you're writing about an event when you were a child, try writing from the viewpoint of your favourite toy, your teddy bear, or your doll. These were your childhood companions who accompanied you on all your adventures.

Write about a specific event from the viewpoint of your chosen toy so that they refer to you in the third person and themselves in the first person: 'I was with John that entire day after the accident, even when he went in the ambulance. I never left his side and I'll never forget the look on his face when ...'

I Never Knew That ...

Sometimes we radically rethink our view of something or someone so that we no longer see things in quite the same way. This can be a very positive experience if our view of the world is enriched and expanded.

Can you think of a time when you had your assumptions shaken, allowing you to see something or someone you thought you knew well in a new light? Try writing about what that was like.

- What did you learn to see differently?
- What difference has that made?
- What happened to change your mind?
- What did you learn from this?

The Secret Life of Emotions

If we are dogged by an emotion like anger, depression or anxiety, we often feel so overwhelmed by it that it overshadows everything we do. Distance yourself from a familiar emotion by writing about it in an objective way. Write about this emotion as if it is an animal.

- What sort of animal would it be?
- What does it feed on?
- Where does it sleep?
- Does it bite?
- What is it afraid of?

For example, if anxiety is an emotion you want to write about, you might write in the following way:

> This is a very nervous fox who runs fast at the first sign of danger, only appears at night and feeds on any prey that falls into its path, especially anxious thoughts which it really loves and gobbles up and gets fat on. It is stealthy and quiet and sneaks up on you when you least expect it. It is always there

in the background, well-hidden but ready to pounce whenever the opportunity arises. It doesn't sleep at night at all or, if it does, it is very restless and roams freely. It is likely to bite anyone who gets in its way or threatens it ....

Writing about familiar emotions like depression, jealousy or anger in this way, using the metaphor of an animal, can help us gain insight into how we really see this emotion. You could try writing in the first person as the animal you have chosen:

I am Freddy the wily fox. I'm very jumpy and highly nervous and I react badly to sudden changes of any kind and most of all I like to stay close to home and my own routine and not to have to take any kind of long journey ....

Put the name of the emotion at the top of the page and then play with it. Try giving it a name. The singer Niall Breslin (also known as Bressie), founder of the website *ALustforLife.com*, wrote a book called *Me and My Mate Jeffrey*. Jeffrey was the name he gave to the depression and anxiety which had been his constant companion for many years. Naming a powerful emotion which has overwhelmed you can also help you to see that you and this emotion are separate, so using the title *Me and My Mate Jeffrey* is a wonderful way of saying Jeffrey may be is a part of my life but he's not me.

Now try writing a dialogue between you and an emotion that dogs you: for example, uncertainty or anxiety or boredom. Write the dialogue the way a play is written, with your own name and the name of the emotion alternating for every second part of the conversation.

> For example:
>
> John: Hi, how are you today?
> Boredom: How do you think I am? There's nothing hap-
> pening as usual.

This exercise helps to create a sense of distance and a greater sense of perspective, especially as such emotions can feel like part and parcel of ourselves. Their effect on our life is so overwhelming and dominant that we can feel ruled by our negative emotions, like a small boat tossed around on a stormy sea.

Writing a dialogue between you and such an emotion can also introduce a sense of lightness, playfulness and even humour, which can go a long way to giving us a sense that, in fact, we are much more in control than we thought.

Through dialogue we can figure things out. Giving powerful emotions an independent voice can help us find what it is they are really trying to express in our life. 'The magic of dialogue is that it goes beneath the surface, tearing away the evident, and bringing forth answer and insights that can help us find a resolution' says Lynda Heines in *Writing Routes*.

Teenage Kicks

In our teenage years we are full of dreams of how our life may unfold. The Melbourne-based theatre company One Step at a Time, working for over two years with a group of young Irish teenagers from Clonmel, created a 90-minute piece of solitary 'journey theatre'. *Forever Young* was designed to raise questions about what happens to youthful dreams, yearnings and ambitions, and how we feel when we look back on our own teenage years. A review of the show at the Edinburgh Fringe in *TimeOut* magazine says:

> *Forever Young* is a beautiful reminder that teenagers are complex beings, that you were one once (remember that?) and that it's best to keep a little bit of that young idealism and rebellion with you, in whatever way you can.

Why not take a journey back in time and encounter your own teenage self?

- Write about an event that happened when you were a teenager. Write from the viewpoint of your teenage self, using their voice and their phrases
- Or write from the viewpoint of your best friend at that time in your life, again referring to yourself in the third person, and using first person 'I' for your friend's voice, e.g. 'Up until we met those boys, Jenny had never even been on a date, let alone kissed anybody. But that night ...'
- Or imagine your teenage self meets up with you as you are today. What would your teenage self say about the person you have become? Try writing the first impressions your teenage self would have of you as you are today.

'It's Just Not the Way I See It'

If you're writing about a conflict with someone at work or with a friend, then try writing in the other person's voice, using their phrases, so they are referring to you in the third person using your name. Try to use the kind of language they would normally use, even if it feels strange at first:

Tony's a good guy but a bit flaky about deadlines and when I realised he hadn't sent the invoice three weeks before, I really hit the roof ...

Writing Slant

If you have a conflict with someone else, instead of writing about how you feel, imagine the other person through the following metaphors:

- If this person was an animal, what kind of animal would they be?
- If this person was a car, what kind of car would they be?
- If this person was a piece of furniture, what kind of furniture would they be?
- If this person was weather, what kind of weather would they be?

Don't overthink your responses. Just write the first thing that comes into your head. Now re-read what you've written and pick the account that suits the most and start writing in the first person as the car, weather or whatever you have chosen:

- 'I am a big grumpy old bear who likes to sit in the corner all day nursing my sore paw ...'
- 'I am a pretty cool leather sofa with soft springs. I like to hang out with people. I like to create a very chilled atmosphere, very smooth. It's important to look well ...'

You can use the same metaphors to look at issues that arise in the organisation you work for or with the team you work in.

The Talking Wardrobe of Clothes

In her book *The Life-Changing Magic of Tidying Up*, Marie Kondo, describing the correct way to fold socks in a drawer, writes that our socks 'take a brutal beating in their daily work, trapped between your foot and your shoe, enduring pressure and friction to protect your precious feet. The time they spend in your drawer is their only chance to rest.'

It's an interesting perspective to take on our clothes. Kondo argues that we should thank our clothes for all the work they do for us. She also says that we should only keep the clothes that truly bring us joy.

Write about some favourite thing you used to wear or still do: a gorgeous dress you wore till it fell apart; a comfortable jumper you put on when you want to be cosy; a favourite tie or jacket.

- What does it feel like to wear it?
- What colour is it?
- What is the texture of the fabric?
- Is it soft and comforting?
- Write about a memory of wearing it.
- Do you still have it?
- Did you give it away?
- If so, imagine a story about someone else wearing it now.

Now write about a specific event where you wore that item of clothing or write about all the good times you've had together, and tell the story from the viewpoint of your dress/jumper/jacket.

The Dog Speaks Up

In the hilarious book *Triggs: The Autobiography of Roy Keane's Dog*, the famous and constant Labrador companion of dog lover Roy Keane, Triggs, writes in the confiding tone of a best friend who advises and counsels his owner during tough times.

- If you have a much-loved cat, dog or budgie, try writing about an event in your life from the pet's perspective.

Or

- Write about how your pet sees you.

No Axe to Grind

Write about something that has made you angry but write about it from a neutral perspective: maybe from the viewpoint of a picture on the wall or a mug on the table, a perspective that has no axe to grind. So, write in the first person, taking the perspective of the picture or mug or table, and write about what you observe in the third person:

It was about eleven in the morning when the whole row kicked off between Noel and Jenny. It was in his office and she came in to ask for the afternoon off and out of the blue he said there was something else he wanted to talk to her about. I could see right away she was completely taken aback when he mentioned her timekeeping ....

Our Experience of Time

Sometimes our experience of time shrinks or expands depending on what is happening in our life, for example, being pregnant or waiting for exam results or serving a long prison term.

> Write about a time in your life when your own experience of time was very acute.
>
> - Were you waiting for something to happen?
> - Was it an unforgettable weekend?
> - Was it a wonderful night out?
> - Or was it waiting for test results?
> - Being trapped somewhere?

Writing through Photographs

Looking at old photographs of ourselves and others stirs up all sorts of emotions and memories.

> Taking such a photograph, write from the perspective of someone else who is in the picture. Write in their first-person voice at the time the photograph was taken.
>
> - What are they thinking about?
> - What are their hopes and dreams?
> - What are they thinking of the other people in the photograph, including you?

Affairs

If the issue you want to write about concerns infidelity in a relationship, first try watching psychotherapist Esther

Perel's Ted Talk on rethinking infidelity, where she challenges the stereotypes surrounding this issue and presents a new framework for understanding relationships.

An affair is usually construed as a pretty black-and-white issue, of the innocent partner and the one who is at fault. In her talk, Esther Perel provides an interesting take on why people might have an affair.

> Try writing about this issue in your own relationship but from the point of view of your partner. Try really going with the flow on this and taking the perspective of your partner.
>
> - What was happening between you two at the time of the affair?
> - What was life like at the time?
> - Why did it make sense to them to do what they did?

Writing Yourself Free

Sometimes we feel overwhelmed by our own life, by the busyness of it, by all the 'stuff' we must take care of. There are some interesting bloggers currently writing about adopting a much simpler, pared-down lifestyle with fewer possessions. Having less stuff to worry about frees up time to focus on what it is you really want to do. Instead of dreaming about all the things you need but can't yet afford, why not flip it and dream about all the things you could cheerfully do without.

> - Try writing about the stripped-down, no frills life. What would it look like?
> - What would you take with you on a long journey if you could only take ten things? Make the list and write about why you chose those things.

6

RESETTING THE COMPASS OF YOUR HEART: VALUES AND GOALS

Have you ever experienced the feeling of being adrift, rudderless, with no map and no destination in mind? The days slip by and you tell yourself that you will get your act together soon and write that book when you get this project finished or learn to swim when your back gets better. For young adults this feeling of being adrift often translates into an expensive series of college course changes and/or dropping out of college. The abject sense of failure only adds to the pain and isolation of not knowing what to do. But this feeling of loss and uncertainty can strike at any age and even stalk us into old age, with conversations tinged with regret for what might have been. A deep sense of disappointment can pervade us if we feel that we somehow did not fulfil our potential. And how did that happen anyway? Where did our lives go?

There is such a strong cultural imperative to live in the now, to seize the day. But if you really don't know what kind of day it is you want to seize, it can be intensely isolating. There is always the challenge of travel or fulfilling our bucket list to soothe our sense that opportunities have passed us by. But seeing Machu Picchu might not solve everything or assuage the dull ache of emptiness when you feel that something is missing from your life.

This chapter is about diving into that sea of confusion and getting to know more about yourself, what makes you tick as a person, what floats your boat. It's about gaining some clarity and doing this now. There is no age or stage at which we cannot embrace change, alter our views, review our lives or change our patterns of thinking.

Nor is changing our lives all about career. It's as much about reconsidering our relationships with our families, our partners, our friends. And to reconsider means standing back, taking stock, slowing down, standing still. It means taking a long pause to breathe and look around and listen to the yearnings we have deep down.

It's only after that stage that we can begin to look at what it is we might like to change or to begin. There is a strong emphasis here on the importance of building daily practices as a way of achieving goals and changing our lives. Building strong daily practices is the best stepping stone to get you to where you want to be or to find out where that might be.

Anchoring Practices

Breathing Space: The Importance of Fallow Time

Letting the ground lie fallow, empty of crops, is an important part of regenerating the soil so that more crops can grow. If you live your life always 'on' – scrolling through Facebook, Twitter or Instagram, constantly checking your phone – fallow time may be a strange concept to get your head around. But if, deep down, you find yourself wishing for something more, if you feel there is a disconnect between what you spend your time doing and what you spend your time dreaming about doing some day, when the time is right, then fallow time may offer the space in which to explore what it is you really want for yourself.

Fallow time is about not having a fixed agenda, it's about leaving space to daydream, to mooch, to wonder, to explore, to trust your own judgement, to get acquainted with your sense of intuition. If you want to see real masters of fallow time, watch anyone under the age of six. They are usually pretty good at just hanging out. In nature kindergartens this idea has really taken root. This global phenomenon in early childcare education began in Norway, based on the concept that children are given a blank landscape of woodland as their playground. Days are spent building dens and climbing trees, exploring their environment and their own capabilities as they develop the skills to create and problem-solve. In outdoor centres, where there is a complete absence of toys to entertain, children still manage to entertain themselves. The absence of a structured play environment doesn't hinder them from having fun and actually seems to foster their ability to figure things out for themselves. In fact, playing outside in nature seems to have huge benefits for children in terms of building their ability to be resilient and independent and to work as part of a team. The adult version of the same thing might be Cheryl Strayed's three-month adventure walking the Great Pacific Highway, which she wrote about in her book *Wild*. The experience changed her fundamentally and helped her to readjust her life course.

But you don't have to take three months off to learn to appreciate the benefits of fallow time. You can go outside, take a notebook, take a wander. Have a day with no agenda.

Let your mind drift. Daydream. Remember what that was like?

Free up some space in which you can listen more to what it is that you long for by spending more time alone. In the words of Martha Postlewaite in her poem 'Clearing', create a clearing in the dense forest of your life. How might you do this?

Stillness

In Eiléan Ní Chuilleanáin's poem 'Swineherd', she writes about listening to cream crawling to the top of the jug. Isn't there an incredible sense of stillness in that line? Listening to cream crawling to the top of the jug. Giving yourself regular doses of slow time is good for thinking about what it is you want to do or be, time in which to unplug and switch off from everything and see what happens. So how might that work for you?

In stillness, we can switch off the endless drone of social media as to 'what's hot/what's not' and just listen to the sound of our own heart, what it longs for. I love one of the things the writer Anne Lamott wrote when she was summarising what she had learned by the age of sixty: 'Almost everything will work again if you unplug it for a few minutes, including you.' So, try unplugging. Unwind; be still and observe what happens then. There aren't many places on the planet where you can't be connected online. But we all need a break from that too. We need silence.

Try spending an hour a day (or whatever amount of time seems to work for you) not being linked to your phone, laptop or tablet. In other words, not checking Facebook or Twitter or newsfeeds or email. Just do nothing. Take a break; unwind from always being 'on'. Loll on the sofa and just let your mind wander. You might begin to see possibilities in areas of your life you have neglected, activities you once loved but abandoned once you got busy. Through being still you might sense more opportunities to be creative, to open up new challenges and aspects of yourself you want to explore. Maybe you might like to paint or take a photography course or dance more. Who knows what might bubble to the surface if you give yourself some time and space in which to let your mind wander without distractions.

Early Morning Routines

In his book, *A Monk's Guide to a Clean House and Mind*, the Japanese Buddhist monk Shoukei Matsumoto points out that we are each composed of the actions we take in life.

Having a good early morning routine makes sense when you think about it. No phones ringing, no emails to be answered. It's a time when you can meditate, write, exercise or do all three. You can use this peaceful time and space to create a sense of stillness and solitude, creating a clearing in all the busyness of our fast-paced 24/7 plugged-in lives. If morning is not a good time for you to work on developing new rituals, you could try developing a set of daily practices at other times during the day.

How can you introduce peaceful quiet routines that foster stillness and solitude? Maybe meditate at lunchtime or take a walk or run then. Write in the evenings. If your life tends to be unpredictable – for example if you work shifts or travel frequently or work unpredictable hours – then build in what you can when you can and don't beat yourself up about not achieving things if it's been a helter-skelter kind of day. If you decide you want to make a change, then do just one thing differently and try to make that a regular thing until it becomes a habit and then you can try introducing another small change. That's how to move things along: slowly altering the course of your life more in the direction in which you have some time for yourself – time to think and be still.

We create our own stories by the day-to-day choices we make. These are the small decisions through which big changes happen, the everyday routines that help to foster our resilience and also achieve the long-term goals. What one small change could you make in your day-to-day routine to achieve something you would like to do?

Find a Mentor

If you already have a clear idea of what you want to do but little idea of how to get there, then consider getting a mentor in that field, someone you admire or aspire to be like someday. A mentor is someone who offers support and guidance. Many successful people are more than happy to share their wisdom and advice with people who are just starting out. And there may be formal mentoring schemes available in your chosen field. For example, writing centres often offer mentoring from successful writers. Or it might be useful to consider getting some life coaching to help you figure out the next steps for you.

Doodling

Try doodling some sketches of what your ideal life would look like in five years' time.

- What would you spend your days doing?
- Where would you be living?
- Who would you live with or would you live alone?

Find Your Tribe

Once you have an inkling about what you would like to pursue, it can be good to connect with like-minded people who can guide you on a path you think might be the one for you. If you have always been drawn to working with your hands, but you work most of the time in front of a screen, then it would be good to connect with a group or a class or do a workshop with people who have similar interests. It can be difficult to continue following a path all on your own with little support from others who don't see the world the way you do or who don't share a common interest. Even if there isn't a like-minded group in your own neighbourhood or city, you might find a group online.

Inspire Yourself

Try finding a quote which inspires you and give it pride of place on your laptop screensaver or pinned to your fridge or bathroom mirror. Pick a quote from someone who really inspires you, a quote that is the epitome of everything you want to bring into your life or into your work; something that encapsulates your dream.

Read

Read to be inspired: blogs, autobiographies, non-fiction accounts of how others reached their goals, perhaps changed direction and found their true path in life. Find out how other people chased their dreams. Reading the stories of how other people found their way towards achieving their goals can give you a sense of not being alone on this quest. It can encourage you to take the first step as well as giving practical advice about how to clarify your own sense of direction.

Writing and Values

And, in all this, there is writing: daydreaming, outlining, planning, tracking. Your writing self, your kind inner mentor, is always on your side, rooting for you to get to where it is you really want to be. It is this inner mentor whom we try to tap into throughout this book and especially here.

Why Writing about Our Goals Works

In her research, American writer Laura King has explored how writing about life goals and ideals led to higher psychological wellbeing (including personal happiness and life satisfaction) as well as fewer visits to the doctor for participants in the five months following her study. People who identify their own internal goals function more efficiently, flexibly and in a more integrated way across all areas of their lives.

Clarifying what our purpose is and what we find personally meaningful makes it much more likely that we will start moving in the direction of achieving our goals. It helps to reduce that wild uncertainty that makes us flounder and doubt ourselves. All we are doing in the exercises here is holding a mirror to ourselves and resetting the compass of our heart.

There are many reasons why writing down your goals is beneficial:

- To give you a sense of purpose, especially about what you want to do in the medium to long term (in the next few months or over the next year)
- To inspire yourself to reach for what you want
- To remind yourself to stay focused and that this is what you really want

- To break down big-picture goals to smaller, achievable steps
- To keep your life organised by tracking on a day-to-day basis what you need to get done in work and in the rest of your life
- To free your mind from endless procrastination and worry: the list is on your laptop, you don't need to have it in your head
- To give focus and purpose so you begin to see a pattern to the things you write down, what it is that you really consider to be important, what you want to give time to, and what is worthwhile – whether that's a daily run or a new work project.

It's probably best to stretch the following exercises out over a period of time. Writing about big stuff like your life direction can take time to figure out so this section is really meant to be something you can come back to, and all the exercises here bear repeating. Our view of what we want from life changes over time so it's always worth checking back with yourself now and again, taking stock.

The Thread

William Stafford, in his wonderful poem 'The Way It Is', describes 'the thread': that goal that may give a sense of purpose to people's lives. The thread is that thing that drives you, what you really love to do. It's where your passion lies. It might be writing; it might be spending time in the great outdoors; it might be fixing up old motorbikes. You'll probably know this thread because when you pursue it you feel centred and content, and when you don't you always have a nagging feeling that something important is missing.

Your thread could be anything at all, but it is usually the thing you would love to focus on if you just had more time.

Try writing about what is this thread in your own life that you must never let go of.

- What do you need to do to focus on it more?
- What is stopping you?

The following two exercises are useful partner exercises to The Thread and form an examination of the recurrent themes in your life.

The List

Pick a time when you won't be disturbed and set your timer for ten minutes. Now, writing quickly and without thinking about it, write a list of all the things that seem important to you. Cover the page, adding new ideas that occur wherever you like. Nobody else will see this list. You can write whatever you like.

Later on, review it. Circle the words or phrases that resonate the most. Finally, draw arrows between things that connect.

The Sound of Your Drum

Sometimes what stops us pursuing what we really want is the idea that what we want makes no sense. There is so much pressure to keep up with the fast-paced existence that most advanced first-world economies espouse in the twenty-first century. There are clear expectations about achieving the predictable milestones in terms of education, career, relationships, family. For anyone who finds it hard to fit in with any of these expectations, it can be difficult to have the confidence to do things differently.

Henry David Thoreau says: 'If a man does not keep pace with his companions perhaps it is because he hears a different drummer. Let him step to the music he hears, however measured or far away.'

- What drummer do you hear?
- What is the music saying?
- Is it loud or is it faint?
- When can you hear this drum beating loudly?

Your Wild and Precious Life

In her poem 'The Summer Day', Mary Oliver, in considering a grasshopper she meets on her walk through the fields, poses the question 'what is it you plan to do with you one wild and precious life?'

This is a big and bold question.

Take some time to write your response. Revisit your writing on this. It may be a work in progress but the question itself is an integral one for long-term goal setting.

Persistence

Sometimes we have a pretty clear view of where we want to go but we lack the energy to stay the course. We fall by the wayside, get distracted by being busy, forget that this is really what we want. I really love the instructions in the poem 'How to Get There' by the Australian poet and cartoonist Michael Leunig, which can be read at his website *www.leunig.com.au*. It's a sort of map of how to stick with something once you begin the journey and open the garden gate.

> Write about stepping beyond your own gate. Where would your journey take you?

Maybe the journey you want to take is a physical journey of travelling someplace or leaving a place behind. But the journey could also be a metaphorical one in which you step beyond the gate, leaving your comfort zone behind. It could mean starting something new, like a course or a relationship. It might be about making a substantial change in the way you live your life.

> What, if anything, is stopping you going beyond your own garden path? Write about what it would be like to take the first steps and then, as in the poem, just keep going, as far as you can see, right to the very horizon.

Dreams to Live By

The haunting lyrics of Ewan McColl's song 'School Days Over', as sung by the irrepressible Luke Kelly of the Dubliners, paints a vivid picture of young dreams thwarted when boys must take their place in the coal pit and leave behind their school days.

> Have you ever had a dream cut short because you had to do your duty? Perhaps you had to take care of an aging parent and gave up a great job. Or maybe you ran out of money for college and had to go to work instead to support yourself. Or maybe you had children while you were very young and had to put your own dreams for career or travel on hold for a while.

- What was it like to lay down your own plan to do something for someone else or for some other reason?
- How did you feel?
- Looking back on that time, what did you learn from the experience?
- Did you get to do what you want in the end?
- If not, what is stopping you now?

Fear of Failing

If you're someone who has a pattern of abandoning projects and plans at an early stage, then this exercise is for you.

Write about what it would be like to succeed instead. What would you need to do?

Begin with the words: 'To keep going and get to where I want to go, I need to ...'

Best Possible Future Self

The following instructions are taken from an experiment conducted by Laura A. King in 2001 in which she asked participants in the study to do the following for four consecutive days:

'Think about yourself in the future. Imagine that everything has gone as well as it possibly could. Think of this as the realisation of all your life dreams. Now, write about what you imagined.'

In this exercise you should try not only to imagine your best possible future but also how you imagine yourself getting there.

- What kinds of things did you do?
- What ways did you behave?

This exercise has been shown to increase personal well-being in terms of happiness and health on a series of measures, so why not try it? It's recommended that you try to write for twenty minutes each day for four consecutive days to explore the value of this exercise fully.

Try writing an email to your future self on the free service *www.futureme.org*. Through this site you can send yourself emails at scheduled times.

Long-Term Goals

- What is the one thing you would like to get done in the next six months to a year?
- What is your dream? Write it out and then ask yourself: why not? Write about why not.
- Is there anyone who can help you? If nobody occurs to you, then write about the ideal person you would like in your corner. Knowing what you need makes it more likely you will recognise it when you meet that person.

Research in positive psychology has found that it's the gritty people – those who ask why not, who give themselves a mantra like 'one day at a time' or who decide that 'failure is not an option' and who surround themselves with people who will be on their side – who are most likely to persevere and win through in the end.

Now what kicker phrase will help you get to where you want? What can you say to yourself over and over to keep going and persevere through the tough times? You might like to fill a page with all the phrases that occur to you. Write them out quickly on one page without thinking about them. Then read them back and pick the one that stands out the most for you.

Weekly Goals

Weekly goals could relate to a project you're working on. Having a written list is a visual reminder every day of their importance. If after a week or so you haven't addressed any of them, take a long hard look at the list and ask yourself the following:

- Are these really the goals I want to achieve?
- Should the list be shorter?
- Should it be different?
- What is stopping me?

Try setting your timer for twenty minutes and write about this last question.

Daily Lists as Living Documents

On a day-to-day basis we need to move from big-picture thinking of long-term goals to how we're going to get there step by step. This is why it can be very helpful to have living documents of daily or weekly goals. Using virtual sticky notes is a constant reminder of these goals.

- Write a list of goals for tomorrow.
- If you're using a laptop or tablet, put these goals on a virtual sticky note on your screensaver so you'll see them all the time.
- Don't make the list too long or the goals too big; just manageable ones that you know you can achieve.

It helps to put the goals in chronological order in terms of when you are likely to do them over the course of the day, or else in order of importance. Then, as you complete each goal delete it.

Going for It

Consider the following, which is a quote about a character from one of the books written by the much-loved American children's writer Beverly Cleary:

> She was not a slowpoke grownup. She was a girl who could not wait. Life was so interesting she had to find out what happened next.

I love the contrast between the description of the 'slowpoke grownup' and the girl 'who could not wait'. The exercise here is to capture what it is like to be excited about your own future, to be endlessly interested in your own life, to let go of the diffidence we acquire as slowpoke grownups and just go for it.

So, try beginning with the words:

- I want to ...
- I cannot wait to ...

Six-Word Memoirs

Ernest Hemingway famously write a poignant six-word short story:

> For sale: baby shoes, never worn.

There have been many attempts since at writing six-word memoirs.

- What is your condensed memoir?
- What six words would you choose to sum up your life?
- How does that feel?

The Memory of Elephants

In 2012 the legendary conservationist Lawrence Anthony died at his home in Thula Thula Game Reserve in Zululand. What happened in the days following his death was truly extraordinary. Two herds of wild elephants grazing in separate areas of the vast reserve began to walk towards his house. Both herds had been saved by Anthony from being shot as pests and had been allowed to live out their lives in peace on the reserve. It took the elephants many hours to make the journey. Neither herd had appeared near the house in over a year and yet from two separate areas of the reserve and within the space of 24 hours both herds arrived and remained near the house for a couple of days. So how did the elephants 'know' that the man who had saved them had died?

There is no logical explanation for this event. The elephants seem to have just 'known' in some ancient inner sense that we all have but often choose to ignore in the face of logic. Some people are better than others at tuning into their 'gut instinct'.

- Do you remember a time when you listened to your gut or followed your heart when it came to making a decision?
- Or was there a time in your life when you chose to ignore your own hunch or gut instinct?

- In either case, write about what happened and how it all turned out for you.

In the Event of Things Going Wrong

In 1995 a 21-year-old Parisian fan of American singer-songwriter Iggy Pop wrote to him. It took Iggy Pop nine months to reply but the day the girl, called Laurence, received his reply, she and her family were being evicted from their flat by bailiffs. If the letter had arrived a day later she would never have received it. The letter is recorded on the website *Letters of Note* and this is part of what he wrote:

> ... most of all I want to see you take a deep breath and do whatever you must to survive and find something to be that you can love. ... i was very miserable and fighting hard on my 21st b'day, too. people booed me on the stage, and i was staying in someone else's house and i was scared. ... so hang on, my love, and grow big and strong and take your hits and keep going.

Write about a time in your life when you managed to hang on and grow strong and take your hits and keep going. What did you learn about yourself from this?

Game Changer

An interesting area of social psychology is the study of what influences and persuades us to change in some way and how we influence others to change. One way of looking at key influences in your life is to look at those moments when you knew that there was no going back.

Something shifted, and you were sure that life would not be the same.

Here's the *Oxford Dictionary* definition of the phrase 'game changer':

> An event, idea, or procedure that effects a significant shift in the current way of doing or thinking about something.

Try thinking of times in your life when an event, idea or way of doing things really stopped you in your tracks and you decided to change your own way of doing something or thinking about something. Maybe a book you read, or an article or blog really struck you and you decided to try out the ideas for yourself. Or maybe you started working with someone whose whole approach made you re-examine your own way of doing things.

- What was the event, idea or way of doing things and what was so different about it?
- What happened then and how did it all turn out for you?

7

Connections

In 1938 a longitudinal study, the Harvard Grant Study, began. Two hundred and sixty-eight male undergraduate Harvard students signed up for the study. For more than seven decades, researchers tracked a range of factors in the men's lives, including intelligence levels, alcohol intake, relationships and income. The findings of this study showed that good relationships are beneficial for our health and wellbeing. Positive close relationships buffered the men from the difficulties in their lives. Being in a securely attached relationship in their eighties helped the men stay sharper in memory. The people who retired happily made concrete efforts to link with new people in their retirement.

In 2012 Harvard psychiatrist George Vaillant, who led the study from 1972 to 2004, published a book on the findings. The study was the only one of its kind, not only because it happened over such an extended period, but also because the men allowed researchers to present their lives in a three-dimensional way in terms of the stories of how their lives had turned out. Doctor Vaillant wrote that there are two pillars of happiness: 'One is love. The other is finding a way of coping with life that does not push love away.'

The importance of our relationships to psychological wellbeing and physical health is backed up by many decades of research. Being socially connected is all about having good positive relationships with others and is strongly associated with feeling happy. The key word here is 'positive'. People who are more socially connected are happier and live longer, but it's the quality of close relationships that matters. For example, even though people in highly conflictual marriages are connected closely to each other, such relationships may be detrimental to health.

Anchoring Practices

Pay It Forward

In 2015 Norma Jean Bauerschmidt was given a tough cancer diagnosis with probably a year left to live. Her doctor offered chemotherapy. Norma looked at him and said, 'I'm ninety years old, I'm hitting the road.' So, she set off on a road trip in an RV with her son, Tim, his wife, Ramie, and a poodle named Ringo. Over the following year, they saw Mount Rushmore and the Grand Canyon. Norma went on a hot air balloon ride, and tried whale watching and ziplining. Her trip was documented on Facebook by Ramie in a page called Driving Miss Norma, and their progress was followed by almost half a million people. When Norma died Ramie suggested that, rather than making a donation or sending flowers, supporters and fans could honour Norma by finding their own ways to 'infuse some joy in the world. Pay it forward in your own community. Pay it forward in your own family. Take your grandmother out for lunch. Heck, take her out for a beer!'

The first suggestion as an anchoring practice in this section on connection is to do just that. In an age when people focus on connection through social media, actual face-to-face connections may become harder to achieve. Reach out to someone and go have some fun with them. Do something for someone else, being consciously kinder in your day to other people. The school principal in R.J. Palacio's *Wonder* used a great phrase in his end-of-year speech, which was 'to be kinder than is necessary'. There is plenty of research to show that doing so will increase your own happiness as well as perhaps making someone else's day.

You're Never Fully Dressed Without a Smile

Try smiling more as you go through your day.

This habit automatically connects you to other people in a positive way and encourages engagement. Smiling has been found to release the happy hormones of dopamine, endorphins and serotonin into your bloodstream, which relax your body and help lower your heart rate and blood pressure. Smiling also has a contagion effect. It's almost impossible not to mirror a baby's smile. When you smile, people treat you differently. You're seen as attractive, reliable, relaxed and sincere. Scientists found that seeing an attractive smiling face activates your orbitofrontal cortex, the region in your brain processing sensory rewards. This suggests that when you view a person smiling, you actually feel that you're being rewarded.

Low-Key Moments of Joy

The Danish word *hygge* describes very ordinary activities in which people come together to spend a little time, maybe for a cup of coffee and some cake or to watch a movie in front of a blazing fire. So, planning something casual – like inviting someone round for cake and coffee – may well be more deeply appreciated by the other person than the grand gesture of perhaps an expensive dinner out because of the very fact that it's easy and relaxed, and there is no pressure to rise to the occasion.

> Consider planning a one-on-one activity with someone you have perhaps been spending less time with lately. This could be an elderly parent, one of your children, or a colleague at work. Just plan something special to do with that person. It doesn't have to be something spectacular. In fact, the more low-key your approach the better because there is less stress and pressure on you to make it all perfect.

Eyes as Windows to the Soul

Making eye contact is a very important way of connecting with other people.

> Watch *Look Beyond Borders: A Four Minute Experiment* on YouTube. Then try really seeing someone when you're engaged in a conversation. Perhaps focus less on what you want to say and instead try focusing on being curious, really trying to perceive the other person.

Reconnecting

In 1994, at the age of 73, Alvin Straight drove his lawn-mower (at five miles per hour) for 240 miles across the states of Iowa and Wisconsin to see his 80-year-old estranged brother, who had recently had a stroke. Alvin had been refused a driving licence as his eyesight was poor.

The journey took six weeks. The David Lynch film *The Straight Story*, based on the story of Alvin Straight, became a critical success. The extraordinary journey is a testament of endurance, love and longing for reconnection.

Since 2000 nearly 20,000 people have participated in twenty rounds of face-to-face reunions between family members who have been divided since the 1950–1953 Korean war. None of the participants had had a second chance to see or talk with their relatives. Over the course of a few days, during which the South Korean families travelled north to meet their relatives, they knew that this would be their one and only opportunity to meet. Many of those who came north had fled from their homes, unaware that the separation from their family would in fact be permanent. More than half of the 132,000 South Korean applicants to the reunions had already died.

> Reconnecting with those who have been important in our lives can be a very positive and often healing experience.
>
> • Is there someone you haven't seen in a long time but whom you would love to see again?
> • What would it be like to reconnect now? With social media it can be surprisingly easy to find people with whom you have lost touch.
> • Are you prepared to take the first step?

Forgiveness

We can spend a lot of energy in our lives holding on to past hurts. How many times have you heard your own angry voice in your head having an imaginary conversation with someone who has hurt you? It can be hard to let go of past hurts, to stop blaming. Sometimes when we forgive someone we see ourselves as perhaps in the lofty role of being smugly right and having the good nature to let the other person off the hook.

Rumi, the thirteenth-century Persian poet, described a neutral place where we can meet: 'Out beyond ideas of wrongdoing and rightdoing, there is a field. I'll meet you there.' This is a place beyond right and wrong, good and bad; a place where we let go of the past and consider where we go from here.

Imagine that you arrive at last into that field. Somebody is coming to join you. It may be someone with whom you have a history, some deep hurt. Perhaps this person is dead, or you are no longer in touch so it's not possible to have an actual conversation. But here you both are in this beautiful field out beyond all ideas of rightdoing and wrongdoing. What is it you would like to say to this person?

Love in Ordinary Times

The poet U.A. Fanthorpe, in her poem 'Atlas', writes a wonderful eulogy to what she calls 'the maintenance side of love'. In most households there is an Atlas figure who holds up the edifice of ordinary day-to-day life. Sometimes this work is so seamless it's almost invisible and so goes unnoticed.

Think about an Atlas figure in your life, past or present.

- What do they do or what did they do?
- How did they do it?

Perhaps consider telling that person how much you appreciate all that they do.

Writing and Connection

Reflecting on our relationships can bring many benefits. It can:

- Help us gain a greater sense of perspective.
- Appreciate the value of what they offer
- Help us deal with loss and grief
- Give us a sense of our own history and connection with our family
- Figure out conflicts

The message from psychological research is clear: relationships and a keen sense of connection with others is important for our wellbeing.

You might try making a list of people in your life – people who have at various times or throughout your life been important to you. The list could obviously include family but also friends, teachers, bosses, work colleagues, neighbours, someone whom you once met on a train, really connected with for a brief time and never saw again – anyone whom you remember vividly as making a significant difference in your life.

So Long, Marianne

In July 2016 Marianne Ihen was dying of cancer, aged 81. She had been the inspiration for Leonard Cohen's songs 'So Long, Marianne' and 'Bird on the Wire'. They had first met on the Greek island of Hydra and spent some very happy years together before separating.

Later in life Marianne described how she had been dreaming of Leonard for 40 years: 'It's always a positive dream.' In a 1992 interview, Cohen said 'When I hear her voice on the telephone, I know something is completely intact even though our lives have separated. I feel that love never dies and when there is an emotion strong enough to gather a song around it, then something about that emotion is indestructible.'

Two days before her death, Marianne received a letter from her former lover, Leonard Cohen, in which he said, 'Know that I am so close behind you that if you stretch out your hand, I think you can reach mine.'

Is there someone in your life – a former sweetheart, lover or friend, someone whom you perhaps have not seen for a long time – who evokes in you that same enduring love described so evocatively by Leonard Cohen?

We may perhaps feel constrained when we consider contacting someone who once meant a great deal to us, someone we still carry in our hearts long after we have lost touch with them. Perhaps we fear the action may be misinterpreted. Maybe old wounds may be reopened. And yet Leonard Cohen manages to reach across the years and speak unflinchingly about love and about death to Marianne.

> If you were to write a final letter to someone in your own life, someone from your past, what would you say?

Flotsam and Jetsam

In 2004 two twelve-year-old French-Canadian girls wrote a message in French, put it in a plastic bottle and dropped it into the St Lawrence River in Quebec. They could hardly have imagined that eight years later a ten-year-old boy in east Cork on the south coast of Ireland would open their bottle and read the message. Thanks to social media and the help of a local newspaper, the boy was able to find the girls, then aged twenty, and they came to Ireland to see their note and meet the boy.

Chance encounters can be wonderful. In Stephen Edgar's poem 'Man on the Moon', he writes of a relationship in which two people's paths have crossed, but that is all. Their paths have carried on in different directions.

Have you ever met someone, even briefly, who left an indelible impression and you have found yourself from time to time wondering 'what if?' Why not write about what that encounter was like:

- Where did you meet?
- What was the weather like?
- What was the light like?
- What else can you remember of that time?
- If you could speak directly to that person now, as Stephen Edgar does in his poem, then what would you say?

Faces

Write about a face you love: someone you see every day or someone who is now dead but whose face you vividly recall.

- What is it about this face that is so special to you? Eyes? Smile? Some familiar expression?

Legacy

This exercise is taken from Marliss Weber in the book *Writing Routes*. I've used this exercise many times in writing groups and it's a wonderful way of seeing both the similarities and the differences from one generation to another.

One of the things I've noticed in doing this exercise is how some legacies skip a generation so that grandmother and granddaughter, for example, are both good at reading maps or love staying up half the night telling stories.

We are all familiar with the expression 'I got that from my father/mother/grandparent'.

From one generation to another we pass on specific skills and interests, whether it's a flair for baking wonderful cakes, or the ability to carve model boats, or a huge knowledge and understanding of theatre.

> - What are the skills, knowledge and interests that you have inherited from your parents or grandparents or someone else of significance in your life?
> - What have these legacies meant to you?
> - What richness have they brought into your life?
>
> Beginning with yourself, write a list of things you are good at or like doing and then pick either your mother or father and write about what they were good at. You could then try writing about your grandmother or grandfather and, finally, try writing the same exercise with your son or daughter in mind or a niece or nephew.

Message in the Sand

On an early morning beach walk I came across the following sentence written in the sand: '... and ... are liars' with the names of two people written in the blanks. I stood and wondered about the writer whose message would only survive for another hour before the tide, then creeping its way up the beach, would wash it away. What anger or sense of abandonment had prompted him or her to make this public announcement? And had it helped to write it?

Writing in the sand ensures that while someone else may see your message, it will soon be washed away forever.

> If you could write just one sentence in the sand on an empty beach right now, what would that sentence be?

Writing the Story of Where You Come From

Psychologists Robyn Fivush and Marshall Duke have explored the value of knowing family narratives for the self-image of children. For example, family stories about parents' experience as children and teenagers help place the child in an intergenerational context. The stories also function to create and maintain emotional bonds among family members. Such stories can extend back to stories about previous generations as well, thus creating a sense of meaning beyond the individual, helping people to see how they are partially defined by the experience of their parents and those of previous generations. Hearing stories from the past can also provide powerful frameworks and perspectives for understanding our own experiences.

> Try writing from one of these prompts:
>
> - What is the most riveting story you heard about your family from your own parents?
> - What is the one story you would like to pass on to the next generation about your family?
> - What is the story that cannot be forgotten?

Childhood

In the film *Boyhood*, a group of four actors were filmed over twelve years by the filmmaker Richard Linklater to capture the journey of the main character, Mason, from a small boy to his first days in college. It manages to record in a stunningly successful way all the little moments that shape the adult he ultimately becomes, and how he reacts and adapts to the circumstances of his life over which, as a young child, he had very little control. Because it was filmed with the same group of actors over such a long time span, the film has a sense of poignancy as we watch through the boy's eyes as he tries to adapt to house moves, new schools and the issues in his parents' lives.

We all have home movie reels in our heads of events in our childhood, and what we may recall as something of huge significance may not even be remembered by others in the family. It's all a matter of perspective.

Why not look at one of your own childhood memories but instead of writing that memory as you remember it try writing about it from the point of view of someone else who was there at the time.

My Mother's Handbag

The following exercise appeared in my previous book, *Writing for Wellbeing*, but I make no apologies for also including it here because in my experience of facilitating writing workshops, this is one of those exercises that captures people's hearts and minds. It's based on the wonderful poem by Ruth Fainlight 'My Mother's Handbag', in which she simply lists the contents of her mother's handbag, but in doing so she also tells us about her life and the kind of person she was. You can hear Ruth Fainlight read the poem herself on *poetryarchives.org*.

You can try this writing exercise in relation to your own mother or, if you're writing about your father, you might describe the kinds of things he carried in his pockets or perhaps the contents of his workshop if he had one.

> The objects we routinely associate with people are very revealing. If you have ever had the experience of clearing and sorting the contents of your family house, you will know all about the poignancy of holding their much-treasured possessions in your hands.
>
> - Why not write about your own mother's handbag?
> - Or the contents of your father's pockets?
> - What sort of things would you be likely to find?
> - What do these things say about her or him?

Did I Ever Tell You You're My Hero?

Who has been a hero or a helper to you? A friend? A teacher, colleague, partner or spouse? It could be someone who inspired you to be the best that you can be or perhaps someone who buoyed you up at a difficult time in your life. Think about how you felt when you were in the depths or when you were struggling to figure things out for yourself.

> Write about who hugged you, listened without judgement, reassured you that they would be there for you, inspired you to be confident.
>
> Write to any of the following writing prompts:
>
> - 'X is my hero because ...'
> - Or write a sent or unsent letter to the person who is your hero.
> - Describe what happened and how this person helped pull you through a tough time.

I'm Still Here

Following his diagnosis with Alzheimer's disease, Glenn Campbell wrote a very poignant love song, 'I'm Not Going to Miss You', to his wife. It's easy to be absent rather than present in a relationship, cruising along on automatic pilot, so we're not really present. It's usually the people with whom we spend the most time whom we are likely to take for granted or feel that we already know everything there is to know about them.

> If you've experienced that kind of drifting away, then what is it you might like to say to your partner or maybe to your child, a parent or a friend?
>
> Try writing the words beginning with 'I'm still here and what I'd like to say to you is ...'

Band of Brothers

The Japanese island of Okinawa is famous for the longevity of its inhabitants. In the documentary *Happy*, a group of elderly women on the island were interviewed. One of them described losing her husband during the Second World War. She had no children but she did have a very strong connection to a group of lifelong friends. They were her family. Soldiers in wartime often describe a similar sense of deep comradeship. The television series *Band of Brothers* depicts this vividly in a group of US troops deployed in Europe during the Second World War.

I once shared an office with two other clinical psychologists who both had a great sense of humour and were liable to break into song at any moment. The job itself involved a lot of travel, long hours driving and working in isolation but coming back to base camp always felt like coming home and there was a huge sense of warmth and humour in that office we shared which somehow got us through. It was the well from which we could draw strength. It's important to be able to find people to connect with to get you through tough times in your life, to help you endure.

> Describe a time in your life when you felt a strong connection to your own band of brothers or sisters.

Home

In his address to accept the Nobel Prize for Literature in 1995, Seamus Heaney recalled the sounds of his childhood home: 'It was an intimate, physical, creaturely existence in which the night sounds of the horse in the stable beyond one bedroom wall mingled with the sounds of adult conversation from the kitchen beyond the other. We took in everything that was going on of course – rain in the trees, mice on the ceiling, a steam train rumbling along the railway line one field back from the house ...'.

> Write about a house you know well: maybe the house you grew up in, a holiday house you go to or went to as a child, your grandmother's house or the house you live in now:
>
> - Describe what this house sounds like: clocks ticking, wind in the trees
> - Describe the smells; cooking smells, farmyard smells
> - The feel of textures; how rough the blankets were, the crunch of leaves underfoot
> - Sights: where was the light and shade in that house? Was it a house full of windows?
> - Tastes: the food you ate then, the sweets you loved
> - Temperature: was it cold or a warm sunny place?

Watching You Shine

In his song 'Father and Daughter', Paul Simon sings about how he is going to watch his daughter shine as she grows up.

> Have you been lucky enough to watch someone shine? It might be precious time with one of your children or grand-children where you got to witness as they took their first steps towards independence or passed an exam they were dreading, got a first job, made a new friend. Write about what that experience meant to you.

Alpha Poem

An alpha poem is a poem in which each new line starts with a letter of the alphabet: so, you write the 26 letters of the alphabet in a column on the left-hand side of a page and then just write something for each letter. The beauty of using a structure like an alpha poem is that each letter is a prompt to write some more. In my experience, it is a structure that most people really like.

> If you are trying to figure out an issue in a relationship, try writing using the letters of the alphabet for each new line of your poem, putting them on the left-hand side of the page and then quickly, and without over-thinking, just write each line beginning with the next letter. Or else write a poem using all the letters of a chosen word, like the name of someone.

Lovely Letters

In 2013 Jodi Ann Bickley set up the campaign and website *One Million Lovely Letters*, in which she began to hand-write thousands of letters to people all over the world. Her book, *One Million Lovely Letters*, became a *Sunday Times* bestseller. Whenever anyone requests a letter, she writes back and sends the letter by post. She said that doing so has not only allowed her to reach out to people who might be going through a particularly hard time in their lives, but it has also helped her to manage her own depression.

Is there someone you know who is going through a hard time at the moment? Try writing what you might like to say to that person if you were to write them a letter.

I'm Really Glad We Got To ...

Some time ago a close friend of mine was dying. A few days before her death, she held a small gathering of her friends in her garden. Even though she could no longer eat or drink, she stayed with us as we had tea. It was a lovely sunny day as she sat enveloped in her rug watching the sky. And then at some point she raised her head and said, 'I want you to remember that right now I am truly happy.' Her death a few days later was deeply sad but I hold in my heart that moment and her words.

Sometimes when someone dies we find ourselves saying things like 'I'm really glad we got to do X'.

Think about such a time in your own life and try writing from the words: 'I'm glad we got to ...'

8

Conclusion

Our life story is the internalised life script that provides meaning and purpose to the *who am I* and *where am I going* stories we all carry round with us. From late adolescence and early adulthood we begin to construe our lives as evolving stories of the reconstructed past and the imagined future in order to make sense of our lives.

I have identified five aspects of positive psychology which have been shown to predict a sense of personal wellbeing and mapped onto these a range of anchoring practices and expressive writing techniques as tools to expand and enrich your own life story.

The anchoring practices are suggestions based on ideas that have emanated both from within and outside the field of positive psychology in terms of establishing routines in your day-to-day life that enhance your own wellbeing. It's down to you to experiment and see what is realistic for you in the context of the day-to-day demands of your life. Even small changes can have a very positive effect in terms of tipping the balance towards the experience of having good days instead of bad ones.

The health benefits of expressive writing have been well established in psychological research. The writing techniques presented here, however, owe much less to psychology and much more to a wider view of creative expression which draws on literature, poetry, metaphor and imagery for its methodology.

Expressive writing nudges you in the direction of writing your own story – a good story, a story of strength, gratitude, tolerance and love – to make it a bigger, better thing that buoys you up.

The nuts and bolts of this book lie in the exercises which I hope you dip into now and then. These are the strands that weave the magic carpet to take you on your journey, to see higher and wider, to see that more is possible.

DELVING DEEPER:
FURTHER IDEAS TO INSPIRE

Chapter 3 – Deeply Appreciating

Listen:

Louis Armstrong singing 'What a Wonderful World'.

Read:

The poem 'The Great Blasket Island' by Irish poet Julie O'Callaghan is a wonderful evocation of the sound memories that a house can hold even if that house is now a ruin.

The poem 'Enough' by Jeffrey Harrison shows how valuable it is to stay in the present moment and notice what is all around in the beauty of nature.

Watch:

Ted Talk by Cesar Kuriyama: 'One Second Every Day'.

In Ireland there's an expression – 'the day that's in it' – meaning the day we have right now. The exercise presented in Brother David Steindl-Rast's five-minute video

'A Good Day' on YouTube is a good exercise to try in terms of daily appreciation of the 'day that's in it'.

Also the short YouTube video 'Life Vest Inside – Kindness Boomerang – "One Day"', created by the founder of *LifeVestInside.com*, Orly Wahba.

Chapter 4 – Developing Flow

Listen:

The documentary mentioned on rally-driving is called 'Roar and Pace' and is part of the *Documentaries on One* series on RTE Radio 1; it can be found on the RTE Doc on One webpage.

Read:

The books I've included here are milestone books on free writing. You might be surprised at the dates of publication: 1934? How could that be relevant? And yet Dorothea Brande's book *Becoming a Writer* (Penguin, 1934), which was published all those years ago, is a joy. It is a book to be savoured, especially by writers who want to develop a regular writing practice to write fiction or non-fiction.

This is a classic work that is especially useful on how to use free writing in timed sessions to stimulate the habit of writing. The ideas presented are based on Brande's creative writing classes. Promotion of the book at the time it was published highlights how it assists would-be writers to harness the unconscious and be their own critics. It's a really well-written useful book on just that.

Natalie Goldberg's *Writing Down the Bones: Freeing the Writer Within* (Shambala, 1986) is an iconic book on writing as meditation. It is packed full of useful ideas and approaches, and is one of the most popular and widely read books on writing. It is an informative book to read on how to use free writing and Natalie Goldberg's voice just jumps off the page with enthusiasm.

The next two books are especially useful if you want to free write but also use this as a way of getting to a polished piece of prose. So, for example, you might want to write an essay or even a book or a proposal. Both books are useful for using free writing to get to the heart of what you want to express and then both present different techniques for fine-tuning what you have written.

Mark Levy's *Accidental Genius: Using Writing to Generate Your Best Ideas, Insight and Content* (BK Publishers, 2010) is very beneficial for writers. Levy looks at how to use free writing to generate ideas by getting beyond your own internal critic. This is a useful book if you want to use free writing in a work context or for generating ideas for a specific writing project or any kind of project really.

Peter Elbow's *Writing with Power: Techniques for Mastering the Writing Process* (Oxford University Press, 1998) is now in its second edition and, like Marc Levy's book, it focuses on using free writing as a method of getting to the best writing, in terms of accessing ideas, a sense of energy and independent thinking, and the sense of your own voice and authenticity in your writing. In Elbow's words, free writing is a bridge between 'felt sense or felt meaning' and language. It's about eventually finding the right words to express what it is you feel through a series of free writes. Elbow's approach is about both encouraging free writing and then a second stage of revising your writing. It's a very useful book if you want to write for work or college assignments or to write a piece for a specific project.

Visit:

Buster Benson's website *750words.com*, based on the Artist's Way morning pages, is a clever idea if you want to try typing your pages each day on a blank screen instead of hand-writing them.

Chapter 5 – Thinking Flexibly

Watch:

The powerful documentary *How to Defuse a Bomb: The Project Children Story* details how an NYPD bomb disposal expert played a key role in helping to defuse tensions in Northern Ireland.

The Nigerian writer Chimamanda Ngozi Adichie's Ted Talk 'The Danger of a Single Story' gives a real insight into how adopting a narrow perspective limits our experiences and how sticking to stereotypes gives us a very unbalanced idea of other people and countries.

Jack Kavanagh's Ted Talk, 'Fearless Like a Child: Overcoming Adversity', is about adopting a positive can-do perspective on adversity.

You can see interviews with David Mach as well as photographs of some of his work on his own website, *www.davidmach.com*. He recently exhibited a very large-scale installation at the 2018 Galway Arts Festival and I was lucky enough to see it. So if you can manage to see his work at an exhibition it is definitely an eye-opening experience.

Read:

R.J. Palacio's book *Wonder* is the story of a boy with a deformed face who goes to school for the first time at the age of ten. It is about his struggle not to be judged on looks alone and for other people to see beyond his deformity to the person he is. It is full of wisdom about how judgements are formed about other people as well as being a remarkable story.

The novel *Olive Kitteridge* by Elizabeth Strout (also now an HBO mini-series) tells the story of a couple from several perspectives. Its layered complexity helps to show how there may be no true version of events but rather different stories depending on the perspective of the narrator.

Chapter 6 – Values and Goals

Explore:

www.selfauthoring.com. This is a website set up by a group of research and clinical psychologists from the University of Toronto and McGill University dedicated to the distribution of tools that improve psychological and physical wellbeing. The self-authoring programme aims to help people explore their past, present and future, and in so doing to become more persistent and engaged in life. Writing about the past, present and future self has been shown to lead to a variety of benefits, both physically and psychologically, including helping to chart a simpler and more rewarding path through life. Writing about an ideal future self shows that goal-setting results in improved productivity and performance.

Read:

Portia Nelson's poem 'Autobiography in Five Chapters' is about getting out of destructive patterns of behaviour. From the book *There's a Hole in My Sidewalk* (Beyond Words Publishing, Hillsboro, 1993).

William Stafford's poem, 'The Way It Is'.

Cheryl Strayed's *Wild: A Journey from Lost to Found* recounts her lone trek along the Pacific Crest Trail.

Jeff Olsen's *The Slight Edge: Turning Simple Disciplines into Massive Success and Happiness* argues that it's not the big monumental changes that matter in our lives but instead it's the small incremental steps we take in terms of developing small positive daily routines that make the difference between success and failure.

Chapter 7 – Connections

Watch:

A beautiful version of Glenn Campbell singing 'I'm Not Going to Miss You' can be seen on *YouTube*.

Watch Robert Waldinger's Ted Talk on the Harvard longitudinal study on happiness, 'What Makes a Good Life? Lessons from the Longest Study on Happiness'.

Or the riveting Ted Talk by George Vaillant on one of the study participants: 'From Emotionally Crippled to Loving Personality'.

The documentary *Happy* on Netflix.

Or you can meet Jodi Ann Bickley in the BBC series *Amazing Humans* and hear her own description of her letter-writing as well as meeting some of the people to whom her letters made a significant difference in their lives.

References

Chapter 1

Csikszentmihalyi, Mihaly (2002) *Flow: The Psychology of Happiness: The Classic Work on How to Achieve Happiness*, second edition, London: Rider.

Dillard, Annie (1989) *The Writing Life*, New York, NY: HarperCollins.

Emmons, Robert (2008) *Thanks! How Practicing Gratitude Can Make You Happier*, New York, NA: Mariner Books.

Isay, David (2015) 'Everyone Around You Has a Story the World Needs to Hear', *Ted Talks*, www.ted.com/talks/dave_isay_everyone_around_you_has_a_story_the_world_needs_to_hear?language=en

Keyes, Marian (2012) *Saved by Cake*, London: Michael Joseph.

Killingsworth, Matthew A. and Gilbert, Daniel T. (2010) 'A Wandering Mind Is an Unhappy Mind', *Science*, Vol. 330, No. 6006, pp. 932, http://science.sciencemag.org/content/330/6006/932.full.

Larkin, Philip (2010) 'Days', *The Whitsun Weddings*, London: Faber and Faber.

Strout, Elizabeth (2008) *Olive Kitteridge*, London: Simon & Schuster.

https://storycorps.org

Chapter 2

Pennebaker, James (1997) *Opening Up: The Healing Power of Expressing Emotions*, New York, NY: Guildford Press.

Robinson, H., Jarrett, P., Vedhara, K. and Broadbent, E. (2017) 'The Effects of Expressive Writing Before or After Punch Biopsy on Wound Healing', *Brain, Behaviour and Immunity*, Vol. 61, pp. 217–227.

Chapter 3

Agroskin, D., Klackl, J. and Jonas, E. (2014) 'The Self-Liking Brain: A VBM Study on the Structural Substrate of Self-Esteem', *PLOS ONE*, Vol. 9, No. 1, e86430, 29.

Berry, Wendell (2018) *The Peace of Wild Things: And Other Poems*, London: Penguin.

Carver, Raymond (1994) 'Gravy', *A New Path to the Waterfall*, reprint edition, New York, NY: Atlantic Monthly Press.

Dante, Aligieri (edited and translated by Mark Musa) (2012) *The Divine Comedy: Inferno*, Vol. 1, London: Penguin Classics.

Dickens, Charles (1836) (New Ed edition, 1995) 'A Christmas Dinner', *Sketches by Boz*, London: Penguin Classic.

Emmons, Robert (2008) *Thanks! How Practicing Gratitude Can Make You Happier*, New York, NY: Mariner Books.

Emmons, Robert and McCullough, Michael (2003) 'Counting Blessings versus Burdens: An Experimental Investigation of Gratitude and Subjective Wellbeing in Daily Life', *Journal of Personality and Social Psychology*, Vol. 84, No. 2, pp. 377–389.

Fredrickson, B.L. (2013) 'Positive Emotions Broaden and Build', in P. Devine and A. Plant (eds), *Advances in Experimental Social Psychology*, Vol. 47, pp. 1–53, Burlington, MA: Academic Press.

Harrington, Gráinne Isobel (2018) 'The Woman Who Redefined Man: Jane Goodall's Life of Activism Continues', *Irish Times*, 7 July.

Hansen, Rick (2008) 'Taking in the Good', *YouTube*, 19 September, www.youtube.com/watch?v=uPXOASa1shY.

Kuriyami, Cesar (2012) 'One Second Every Day', *TED Talks*, March, https://www.ted.com/talks/cesar_kuriyama_one_second_every_day.

Matsumoto, Shoukei (2018) *A Monk's Guide to a Clean House and Mind*, London: Penguin.

Pancake, Breece D'J (2014) 'Trilobites', *Trilobites and Other Stories*, London: Vintage Books.

Saki (H.H. Munro) (1976) *The Best of Saki*, London: Pan Books.

Simons, Daniel (1999) 'Invisible Gorilla', www.theinvisiblegorilla.com and www.youtube.com/watch?v=vJG698U2Mvo.

Toepfer, Stephen and Walker, Kathleen (2009) 'Letters of Gratitude: Improving Wellbeing through Expressive Writing', *Journal of Writing Research*, Vol. 1, No. 3, pp. 181–198.

Walcott, Derek (1992) 'Love after Love', *Collected Poems, 1948–1984*, new edition, London: Faber and Faber.

Chapter 4

750words.com.

Becomingminimalist.com.

Brande, Dorothea (1991) *On Becoming a Writer*, revised edition, New York: Jeremy P. Tarcher.

Csikszentmihalyi, Mihaly (2002) *Flow: The Psychology of Happiness: The Classic Work on How to Achieve Happiness*, second edition, London: Rider.

King, Stephen (2000) *On Writing: A Memoir of the Craft*, London: Hodder and Stoughton.

Loud TV (2014–) *Tiny House Nation*.

Trichter Metcalf, Linda and Simon, Tobin (2002) *Writing the Mind Alive: The Proprioceptive Method for Finding Your Authentic Voice*, New York, NY: Ballantine Books.

Chapter 5

Aitchison, John (2016) *The Shark and the Albatross*, London: Profile Books.

Alleycats Films (2016) *How to Defuse a Bomb: The Project Children Story*.

Bolton, Gillie, Field, Victoria and Thompson, Kate (eds), *Writing Routes: A Resource Handbook of Therapeutic Writing*, London: Jessica Kingsley.

Breslin, Niall (2015) *Me and My Mate Jeffrey*, Dublin: Hachette Ireland.

www.davidmach.com.

Howard, Paul (2012) *Triggs: The Autobiography of Roy Keane's Dog*, Dublin: Hachette Ireland.

Kondo, Marie (2014) *The Life-Changing Magic of Tidying Up*, London: Vermilion.

Langer, Ellen (2010) *Counterclockwise: A Proven Way to Think Yourself Younger and Healthier*, London: Hodder and Stoughton.

Milne, A.A. and Shepard, E.H. (2016) Winnie *the Pooh: The Classic Collection of Stories and Poems*, London: Egmont.

Pennebaker, James (1997) *Opening Up: The Healing Power of Expressing Emotions*, New York, NY: Guildford Press.

Perel, Esther (2015) 'Rethinking Infidelity ... A Talk for Anyone Who Has Ever Loved', *Ted Talks*, www.ted.com/talks/esther _perel_rethinking_infidelity_a_talk_for_anyone_who_ has_ever_loved.

www.tarabrach.com.

Time Out (2015) 'Forever Young', *Time Out Edinburgh*, 22 August, www.timeout.com/edinburgh/theatre/forever-young.

Chapter 6

Cleary, Beverly (1968) *Ramona the Pest*, New York, NY: Harper Collins.

Iggy Pop, 'Hang On My Love, and Grow Big and Strong', *Letters of Note*, 15 January 2010, www.lettersofnote.com/2010/01/hang-on-my-love-and-grow-big-and-strong.html.

King, Laura (2001) 'The Health Benefits of Writing about Life Goals', *Personality and Social Psychology Bulletin*, Vol. 27, No. 7, pp. 798–807.

Leunig, Michael (no date) 'How to Get There', *Leunig.com*, www.leunig.com.au/works/poems.

Matsumoto, Shoukei (2018) *A Monk's Guide to a Clean House and Mind*, London: Penguin.

Ní Chuilleanáin, Eiléan (1991) 'Swineherd' in *The Second Voyage*, Winston Salem, NC: Wake Forest University Press.

Oliver, Mary (1990) 'The Summer Day', *House of Light*, Boston, MA: Beacon Press.

Postlewaite, Martha (no date) 'Clearing', *Habits for Wellbeing*, www.habitsforwellbeing.com/clearing-by-martha-postlewaite/.

Stafford, William (2006) 'The Way It Is', *New and Selected Poems*, Minneapolis, MN: Graywolf Press.

Strayed, Cheryl (2012) *Wild: A Journey from Lost to Found*, New York: Alfred A Knopf.

Chapter 7

Bickley, Jodi Ann (2014) *One Million Lovely Letters*, London: Hodder and Stoughton.

Bolton, Gillie, Field, Victoria and Thompson, Kate (eds) (2011) *Writing Routes: A Resource Handbook of Therapeutic Writing*, London: Jessica Kingsley.

Campbell, Glenn (2015) 'I'm Not Going to Miss You', on *Glenn Campbell: I'll Be Me Soundtrack*, Big Machine Records.

Duke, M.P., Lazarus, A. and Fivush, R. (2008) 'Knowledge of Family History as a Clinically Useful Index of Psychological Wellbeing and Prognosis: A Brief Report', *Psychotherapy: Theory, Research, Practice, Training*, Vol. 45, No. 2, pp. 268–272.

Edgar, Stephen (2006) 'Man on the Moon', *Other Summers,* North Fitzroy, Vic: Black Pepper.

Fanthorpe, U.A. (1995) 'Atlas', *Safe as Houses,* Cornwall: Peterloo Poets.

Lynch, David (1999) *The Straight Story,* Walt Disney Pictures.

McAdoo, Patricia (2013) *Writing for Wellbeing,* Dublin: Currach Press.

Netflix (2011) *Happy.*

Playtone, DreamWorks Television and HBO (2001) *Band of Brothers.*

Simon, Paul (2006) 'Father and Daughter' on *Surprise,* Paul Simon.

Vaillant, George (2015) *Triumphs of Experience: The Men of the Harvard Grant Study,* Cambridge, MA: Harvard University Press.